The Marriage Pyramid

Pathway to a Godly Marriage

Danny B Purvis, PhD

The Marriage Pyramid
Copyright © 2018 A Growth Project Publication

Growth Project is a virtual discipleship ministry platform designed to help individuals and organizations develop and implement unique discipleship paradigms. We offer a variety of learning opportunities, leadership training, marriage seminars, and resources to assist in the process of growing in Christ. For a complete listing of our programs and resources, please refer to www.growthproject.org.

ISBN 978-0-578-42175-9
1. Christian Marriage. 2. Family Relationships
3. Theology 4. Religion 5. Christianity

Table of Contents

Foreword   4

Chapter 1 **PERSPECTIVE**   8

Chapter 2 **LOVE**   32

Chapter 3 **SAFETY**   54

Chapter 4 **GROWTH**   89

Chapter 5 **ONE**   121

Chapter 6 **ODDS AND ENDS**   170

Chapter 7 **GROWTH PROJECT**   185

Foreword

I was a Navy Chaplain for 20 years. I don't tell you this in order to suggest that this in any way comes close to identifying me. It doesn't. I simply tell you this because the genesis of the Marriage Pyramid idea began during my time in the Navy. In fact, I stumbled upon this idea while taking part in my first marriage seminar in my first duty station while stationed in Twentynine Palms, California in 1999.

I had never participated in a marriage seminar before, and I really wasn't quite sure what to do. At the time, my wife and I were about to celebrate our 10th wedding anniversary, and so I figured I must have learned something about marriage in that decade. Looking at the material we were supposed to present to these newly married couples, I discovered that the info, while fine enough, simply lacked something. It lacked accessibility.

What do I mean by that? I mean that while the information was sound, and the precepts were solid, I wondered how much of this stuff people were actually going to remember so they could then put it into practice. Instead, I wanted a picture, an image of some sort that not only conveyed the depth of the principles I envisioned but also the simplicity in how these principles were connected. I wanted to illustrate what an optimal marriage looks like. Notice, I didn't say what an ideal marriage looks like. Because in my experience, there is no such thing as an ideal marriage. Not with our skewed perception of reasonable expectations.

The Marriage Pyramid seemed to be an ideal approach to satisfy both of those requirements. Thus, the Pyramid was born. Not in the form in which you will see it described in this book, but in a much more complete and (hopefully) understandable way. I wanted a paradigm that revealed the complexities of what it takes to have an optimal marriage. I also wanted it to be accessible to those who actually want an optimal marriage.

That's why I started out by telling you that I was a Navy Chaplain for 20 years. This idea was planted, watered, fed, and harvested during the myriad of marriage seminars I led while in the Navy. In fact, at my last duty station, my entire job was to organize, develop, and lead marriage retreats within the context of the Navy's retreat program known as CREDO. The last year and a half I spent in the Navy was solely dedicated to doing marriage retreats for young (and sometimes not so young) married Marines and Sailors. I conducted dozens of retreats for hundreds of couples. And I loved every bit of it.

This book, *The Marriage Pyramid*, is the culmination of all of those years leading all of those seminars. It is the culmination of all of the marriage counseling I performed for a multitude of couples desperate to find a way to make their marriage work. It became a bit of an obsession for me. I wanted the joy I had in my own marriage to be transferred to the couples I counseled. I wanted to tell them to hang in there, just look at it a bit differently, and don't give up hope. Unfortunately, too many of these couples did just the opposite.

That is also the reason for this book. Marriage holds a special place in the heart of God. It was the first institution He ever created. It even predates the establishment of the church. It is a precious and amazing commodity that not only benefits the people involved in the marriage but also the culture at large. Failed marriages are not good for anyone. It is my prayer that this book will help, in some small way, to fix this problem. God loves marriage. He has provided a blueprint for what He intended marriage to be in His Word. It is sacred, and it is precious. And it is in trouble in more ways than we can imagine.

So that is the impetus for writing this book in the first place. There have been many people along the way who have been instrumental in seeing this completed. I am indebted to all of them, but can in no way thank each and every one of them. But I will try.

I would like to thank all of the folks that attended the CREDO Marriage Enrichment Retreats over the years. I can't tell you how much your encouragement meant to me, especially where the Marriage Pyramid was concerned. That part of the retreat always garnered the most input and positive response. This led me to believe that I was really on to something with this program. Many times, after the Marriage Pyramid session was complete, I would have multiple participants ask, "When are you going to write a book about this?" Well, the answer to that question is: right now. Thanks for helping me see value in this paradigm.

More importantly, I want to thank my wife, Kimberly. At the writing of this book, we have been married for 29 years. We actually met, however, when we were six years old and in the same first grade class. Every time I have doubted myself over the years which has been often, she was the one who believed for the both of us. If I could have sat down and designed the perfect wife before I married, I could not have come up with what Kimberly has been to me. I have known her for 47 years. I can't remember a time in my life when she wasn't in some part of it. When people ask what it means in Genesis when God states, "And they shall become one flesh" (Gen. 2:24), I wish that for just one second (that's all they would need) they could switch places with us. Then that question would be answered. None of what I have ever accomplished or will ever accomplish would have happened without you. I don't know what I can say except… thank you. From the depths of my soul… thank you.

And, most importantly, to my Lord and Savior, Jesus Christ, I give more thanks than I can say. He reached into the life of a wayward, rebellious enemy and bestowed grace I did not deserve. Anything good that comes out of my life, He is responsible for. Any good that the Marriage Pyramid might do is all because of Him. I am so thankful that He didn't see fit to make me a better person. Instead, He made me a completely new person. A person who wears the cloak of righteousness that rightfully belongs only to Him. If I live 1,000 lifetimes, I will never deserve the grace He bestowed upon me that began in a manger and ended in an empty tomb.

So if you've gotten this far, congratulations. Virtually no one (except maybe the author's friends and family) ever takes the time to read the foreword. I don't know if that is a good thing or not. But I felt it necessary to let you know a little about the background of this idea and how it has developed. I will go into more detail about all of this as we wind our way through the book. I hope you find it helpful. I hope you will see marriage in a way that you've never seen it before. Most importantly, I hope that you will see marriage as a precious gift from a God who loves us more than we could ever dream.

Whether this ends up being a worthwhile endeavor… I leave that to you. Are you ready to get started? Then let's go.

Chapter One
PERSPECTIVE

Call me old-fashioned, but I have always felt that in order to truly get to where you want to be, you have to understand from where you came. When I was in the Navy, people used to constantly ask me: "What do Navy chaplains do?" For years, I never had a very good answer to that question. It really depended on what type of unit I was in, what type of Commanding Officer I had, and what kind of job I held. At any given time, people wanted me to be a social worker, a priest, a pastor, a counselor, a resource, or a get out of jail free card. And those roles just scratch the surface of the expectations that were placed on me. I didn't mind though. It did lead to a great deal of vocational schizophrenia at times.

Later on in my career, I came up with a much better, pithier, and comprehensive answer to that question. When asked, I would then answer: I provide perspective. As strange as it may sound, I began to see myself as someone who could provide a way of seeing things completely different than the way the person sitting across from me saw them. If someone was struggling with something and was getting advice from a worldly perspective, I would give them the Biblical perspective. If someone was struggling with a relationship, I gave them an alternate way of looking at things, and so on.

In fact, it became so that I would count a counseling session as successful if I heard the person at some point in our conversation say, "I never thought about it that way before." Perspective is everything. I usually do not completely agree with what could be seen as hyperbolic truisms, but with this one I do.

The way in which we view anything in our lives determines what value we place on that thing. It also informs our perception of that thing, whether the perception is correct or not. Perhaps my perspective joke will provide, well… some perspective: "What did the snail say while he was riding on the turtle's back? Wheeeeeee!"

To us, the turtle is very slow. To the snail, it's the fastest he (or she) has ever gone. Besides being a very bad joke, the witticism has a point. The point? Perspective is everything. That is the purpose of this chapter. We are going to provide a different perspective regarding some of the elements of marriage that have been misappropriated and misused for years. In order to see what God's design for your marriage is, we have to see the misconceptions that have been implanted in your heart and your mind regarding marriage. Many of the issues raised in this introduction will be examined much more closely as we make our way through the book. Some of them will just be exposed and discussed here, but the goal is to provide a perspective on some aspects of marriage that differ from the culture's often false and always skewed view of this sacred institution. As I said, the only way we can see something for what it truly is, is to correct the errant presuppositions and clarify the false perceptions that surround it in the first place. That's what we're going to do now.

Why is there conflict in the first place?

It's not exactly breaking news to claim that there has always been and will always be conflict between husbands and wives. Of all the counseling I did as a Navy Chaplain (and that was a lot), the vast majority of that counseling was done with couples who were struggling with their marriage. It is not an exaggeration to say that, over 20 years, I counseled hundreds of couples representing hundreds (maybe thousands) of people. I did enjoy marriage counseling, though it could get a bit trying at times. This is not a criticism, but it is an observation: most couples thought they were "due" a happy marriage. Simply by virtue of being married. I quickly came to the conclusion that most couples thought they could have a 30-year marriage in year 4, which led them to make one of the most fatal mistakes a married couple can make with regards to their marriage: they actually believed their own unrealistic expectations. I will have a lot more to say about this almost universal problem that plagues virtually every marriage. Suffice it to say, for now, that you just need to take my word for it. The most prevalent fatal problem I have ever encountered in marriages is unrealistic expectations. And every single married couple on the planet suffers from this malady. We'll talk about how we fix this problem later. For now, it's enough for you to know how devastating it is.

However, convincing couples of this truth was often difficult in light of the fact that it sounds "too simple," and it doesn't fit the template the culture provides regarding marriage. Therefore, I knew I would have to ask the right questions if I wanted to get the right answers. So I began asking these military couples a question I knew they would answer in such a manner that would lead them to the truth. I asked them, "In the Navy, in your job, when do you stop training?" The answer, of course, was always the same. They would gleefully respond that, in preparation for their military job, they would never stop training. I would ask them, "How long will your military career last?" They would generally say things like 4, 10, 20 years.

I would then shift gears and ask, "How long are you supposed to be married?" After convincing them it was not a trick question, they would answer, "Forever." I then would ask the most important question: "How much training do you get for that?" Then you could see it. The light dawning in their eyes, as what I was trying to show them was becoming real. There are two ways we can communicate a truth. We can simply declare the truth claim, or we can ask the right questions so that the person comes to the truth claim on their own. I prefer the latter. That way, the person owns the knowledge because they used the questions to find their way to the truth instead of simply being told.

In this case, the truth they came to was this: they acknowledged that that, in their job, they would receive non-stop training for an endeavor that might only last 4 years. On the other hand, they then acknowledged that they had virtually no training for marriage, which is supposed to last a lifetime. Just as their eyes were opened by seeing what I often call the "thing behind the thing" (we'll get into this in much more detail later), so do our eyes need to be opened to see exactly what the foundation is for conflict in all marriages today. There is an answer to that question. And it is an answer that is apropos to every single marriage that has ever existed. To see this answer, we have to take a trip back to Genesis.

In the beginning

The first three chapters of Genesis are so extraordinary that they cover everything from the creation of the universe to the fall of humanity. And that's just in three chapters! With so much going on it is easy, even with a close reading of the text, to miss something that is of the utmost importance if we are to truly understand the genesis (pun intended) of all conflict in every single marriage on the planet, including the first marriage. I am not going to win the Pulitzer by simply relaying to you that, historically, there have been a few issues between husbands and wives. But maybe if I can show you the origin of these problems, just maybe, it will go a long way to helping us alleviate some of them.

The Fall is the penultimate event in human history. From the moment of Adam and Eve's sin, the framework for the Crucifixion, Resurrection, and Second Coming was being completed. When God is pronouncing His judgement as a result of this first sin, He states, "I will put enmity between you and the woman, and between your seed and her Seed; He shall bruise your head, and you shall bruise His heel" (Genesis 3:15). In that last statement, God clearly alludes to the Crucifixion ("you shall bruise His heel") and the resurrection and ultimate victory of the Second Coming ("He shall bruise your head"). After reading the details of the creation followed quickly by the first human sin and then immediately followed by the consequences for that sin, it would be completely excusable if we miss the origin of the tension between husbands and wives that leads to so much consternation and difficulty. And the origin of all marital strife is, as so many problems are, rooted in sin.

After the Fall, God begins to immediately hand out a series of punishments to Adam, Eve, and Satan that, of course, would then be passed to all of humanity from that point onward. Some of these are more well-known than others, but there is one that is often more overlooked than others. In the latter part of Genesis 3:16, the text reads: "Your desire shall be for your husband, and he shall rule over you." The reason this passage is extremely misunderstood stems from, I believe, the misunderstanding of a word that the average English reader might simply skip over. The word in question is "desire". Herein lies the problem of translating other languages into English. Oftentimes, a word is used in translation that could easily be misunderstood as it relates to its true meaning.

For example, desire in a marriage does not seem like a negative thing. In fact, if I am to "become one flesh" (Genesis 2:24b) with my wife, then I would think that desire would be a good thing. I desire my wife. I desire her love, affection, and attention. She desires me in the same way. Yet in the middle of the judgements being pronounced by God after the Fall, it seems to suggest that desire is a punishment. How could this be? The answer lies in not simply looking at the English translation but in what the word truly means in context. In understanding the Bible, context might not be everything, but it's pretty darned close. Because, in reality, we know that desire in and of itself is not a bad thing. In fact, read Song of Solomon, and tell me the author does not desire his wife. Desire drips from many of those pages. However, we see what this word in Genesis actually means by looking at another example of the same word. And that word is found just one chapter over.

Genesis Chapter four begins with the all too familiar and tragic story of Cain and Abel. We know the end of the story. We know that Cain ends up committing the first murder ever recorded when he murders his brother Abel in cold blood. We may not know, however, that God tries to warn Cain earlier in the story. And He uses familiar verbiage. God cautions Cain by stating, "And if you do not do well, sin lies at the door. And its desire is for you, but you should rule over it" (Genesis 4:7b). Did you see the familiar verbiage? God stated that sin was awaiting Cain and that it *desired* him. This is the exact same word and the exact same grammar that was used in Genesis 3:16b when God told Eve her *desire* would be for her husband. Therefore, we have to use Genesis 4:7b to help us get to the essence of Genesis 3:16b. God does all of the work for us; we just have to follow the truth.

God not only tells Cain that sin desires him; He also tells Cain what sin wants to do. Simply put, sin wants to rule over Cain.

That is precisely why God tells Cain that he must instead "rule over it." Therefore, the word *desire* used in conjunction with Cain and sin is not a good word at all. It is not the type of desire we are to have for our relationship with our spouse. And that is exactly why the same word was used in Genesis 3:16b with Adam and Eve. If this is the same word with the same meaning (and it is), then what God was actually saying to Eve was: your desire will be to rule over your husband (similar to sin's desire to rule Cain), but instead he will rule over you. And what happens when one person rules, but someone else thinks they should rule? Simply put: issues.

Do you see what is at work here in concert with marital strife? As I stated earlier, it is not breaking news that all marriages suffer from strife, discord, or calamity. It happens all the time. It has happened in your marriage. And if you're reading this and you are not married, I have some bad news for you: strife and difficulty will strike your future marriage as well. It cannot be avoided because it is rooted in sin. And we all struggle with sin (Romans 3:23). Why am I telling you this? In the famous book trilogy *The Hunger Games*, there is an interesting phrase that is used in the second novel, *Catching Fire*. While trying to convince the main protagonist, Katniss Everdeen, that he means her no harm, potential enemy Finnick Odair tries to reassure Katniss that he is on her side by stating, "Remember who the real enemy is."

That is exactly why I am taking time in this introduction to show you the origin of marital dysfunction and how it relates to our ultimate adversary, Satan, who introduced us to sin in the first place. In the middle of fights, arguments, and strife with our spouse, it is extremely tempting and easy to see that spouse as our enemy. I want X, my wife wants Y, and I struggle and argue with my wife to get what I want. She struggles with me to get what she wants. In this scenario, my tendency is to see my wife as an enemy that must be conquered. After all, the goal of an argument is to win. It is then that I must hearken back to this truth: remember who the real enemy is.

My spouse is not my enemy. The problem is the enemy. The adversary, Satan, is my enemy. Isn't it interesting that marriage was the first institution created by God and that it was immediately attacked by Satan? When Adam was alone prior to Eve's creation, Satan was nowhere to be seen. Only after the first marriage was consecrated was there the first attack on that marriage. And the attacks have not subsided. Nor will they ever. We will go into much more detail concerning these issues as we unpack the Marriage Pyramid. However, it was most important that I make sure we had our presuppositions correct about the origin of conflict and strife in marriages today and that it all started in a Garden. This reality, of course, leads us to another quick foundational element related to this idea that plagues both Believers and non-believers alike regarding the Biblical view of the marriage relationship.

To submit or not submit, that is the question.

I have long maintained that every non-believer knows at least two Scripture verses. The first is: "Judge not lest ye be judged" (Matthew 7:1). And the second one is: "Wives, submit to your own husbands, as to the Lord" (Ephesians 5:22). It is interesting. The very reason both of those are so well known among non-believers is due to the fact that they are drastically misunderstood among non-believers. To be honest, these verses are also among the most misunderstood even by those who profess faith in Christ. Hopefully, we can at least clear up this one verse. Let's give it a try.

The first thing we have to get straight, if we are to ever truly understand what God is saying here, is what "submit" really, actually means — the Biblical understanding of what this construct actually means, as opposed to what people say it means. First, in order to best understand what God is trying to say here, it must be noted that the word "submit" does not even appear in verse 22. The command in verse 22 is a continuation of a command to submit that appears in verse 21. Interestingly, Ephesians 5:21 states that we should, as Believers, submit: "to one another in the fear of God". This verse concludes a section of Scripture where Paul admonishes all Believers to submit to one another. This command is in keeping with the idea Paul discusses in Galatians when he states, "There is neither Jew nor Gentile, neither slave nor free, nor is there male and female, for you are all one in Christ Jesus" (Galatians 3:28). We harken back to this because this idea of Believers submitting to each other, regardless of their social or cultural position, shows that there is no favoritism with God. He does not view some Believers as less important or less valuable than others. We submit to one another because we are all equal in worth. We are not, however, all equal in the role God has for us. Therein lies the problem.

We hear the word "submit," and we immediately think that the person submitting has to be of lower worth or value than the one being submitted to. While that may the case in the world, we are not talking about the world's way of doing things. In the original language, the word translated as "submit" is the word "hupotasso," which literally means "to place in an orderly fashion" (Zodhiates, 1427). That's it. That is all the word means. It is just a way to place things in an orderly fashion that has nothing at all to do with the worth or value of the things being placed. God knew (of course He did) that without order things immediately devolve into chaos. Again, the marriage relationship was the first institution

God ever created. He desperately did not want that institution devolving into chaos, especially in light of the sin problem we mentioned above that would certainly lead to that inevitability.

Interestingly, the one secular example I can use that might go a little way towards explaining this so that we can understand it comes from the military. The military is probably the most structured organization on the planet. Everything is ordered and regimented. Competent leadership is needed at every level of that organization. In order to help accomplish that, there is a rank structure. The ranks are broken down into two basic groups. You are either an officer or an enlisted person. And the primary way an enlisted member recognizes an officer is to render a salute when the time is warranted. The enlisted person, being of lower rank, initiates the salute, and the officer returns the salute. A lower ranking officer will initiate a salute to a more senior officer. That's the way it goes. People both inside the military and outside the military have often viewed this custom in the wrong way.

The salute is simply a reminder of the order that is prescribed by the military. It is not an act that suggests, in any way at all, that the person receiving the salute is superior in worth as a human being. They have a superior rank, and role, in the institution. But they are not a superior person. I have had to tell folks who have an issue with this that when you salute, you are saluting the rank, not the person. In fact, the person you are saluting may be, personally, the worst person on the planet. How do I know if the person I am saluting is actually a child molester? I don't. But my salute is not acknowledging that the person I am subordinate to in position is a better person than me (depending on how you define that). I am merely acknowledging the order prescribed by the institution so that the institution does not deteriorate into chaos.

This is very similar to the role of husband and wife. God has ordained that the husband be in the position of leadership. That does not mean that he is the "better" person. It does not mean that God values the husband more than the wife. It does not mean that God thinks that the husband is of more worth. We know this from the Galatians passage mentioned above (among many others). God does not want His institution falling into chaos. He did the same thing for His other prized institution: the church. He notes that pastors and elders play a different role than the "average" Believer (1 Timothy 3:1-13). They are in a role that involves a certain amount of authority. However, that does not mean that God values them or views them as more worthy than others. He ordained things like this so that order can be kept in two of His most precious institutions: the church and marriage.

Still not buying any of this? Let me propose a series of statements. I then want you to think about what our society today would say about a woman making statements like these. Here they are:

"My husband is greater than me."

"I can't do anything of myself, I only do what I see my husband do."

"I don't do what I want to do, only what my husband tells me to do."

"I don't say anything on my own, only what my husband tells me to say."

"I make myself nothing compared to my husband."

Again, let me ask the question I posed above: what would be the reaction in our culture today to a wife who made those statements? What would be the reaction today by some Believers to a wife who made those statements? Do any of those statements sound a bit familiar? I hope they do. All of those statements were made by Jesus. All I did was change the word "Father" to "husband". Here are the Scripture references for each of those statements in order: John 14:28; John 5:19; John 6:38; John 12:49;

Philippians 2:5-8. See what I am getting at here? Jesus was in a role as the Incarnated Christ to be submissive to the will of the Father, a role He gladly held. And yet He is God. The second Person of the Trinity. He created everything (John 1:1-3). And He was submissive to the Father. Does that make Jesus of less worth than the Father? No. Does it make Him less valuable than the Father? No. Does this submissive role change the essence of Who Jesus is at all? No. That's why Jesus was able to do what we find so difficult as His followers, and that is submit.

This example is 100% apropos to what we are seeing here with the command for wives to submit to their husbands. It actually makes me very angry when we see such a beautiful picture of what true, unadulterated submission really looks like for all Believers but ignore it because we would prefer to listen to the world's perspective on this rather than God's. Do we not believe Jesus' words? "You will be hated by everyone because of Me" (Matthew 10:22). The world hates us because we love God (John 15:18-25). Since that is the case, why then do we listen to the world's assessment of what God thinks about husbands, wives, and marriage in general? The world will tell you that God thinks wives are second-class citizens. The world will tell you that God values husbands more than wives. The world will tell you that you need to see your spouse as your adversary, designed only to keep you down. And you're going to listen to a group of people who hate you? It boggles the mind, but it happens. Hopefully this brief look at what true, Godly submission looks like will help end this foolishness and get us better oriented for the rest of the book and how we can have the marriage God wants us to have.

But besides the origin of strife and the misunderstanding of God's order with regards to marriage, what other foundational presuppositions do we have to get right before we move on? I would say it is one that is the most visible and yet the most overlooked. And that is the role personality plays in all of this.

Are we just wired this way?

Throughout my many marriage counseling sessions, one of the most familiar and oft-repeated claims from both partners would be the surety they had in thinking the annoying traits of their spouse had to be intentional. In other words, the vast majority of times, I would hear complaints from one spouse about the other, only for the complaining spouse to conclude that "he only does this to annoy me" or "she knows how much I hate it when she does this." The implication is clear. All of the irritating personality quirks inherent in every single human being are being exhibited for the sole purpose of annoying our spouse.

To be sure, there are times when this is true. If I am particularly put-out with my spouse, I am ashamed to admit that I might, from time to time, engage in a behavior that I know will irritate her. As much as I love her, if she exasperates me enough, I am not above a little sin-inspired behavioral revenge. However, my experience, both in my own life and in listening to other couples, is that the vast majority of my peculiar, irritation-inducing behaviors have nothing to do with vexing my wife. They are, for lack of a better term, simply how I am wired.

Throughout my years of leading marriage seminars, I have adapted and improved the material I present. The very last retreat I led was drastically different from the very first one. As I discovered new insights or was made aware of more tools, I often replaced some modules with those that I felt were more beneficial. However, there are quite a few elements that have remained unchanged since day one. One of the most useful tools I have used and continue to use is explaining the role that personality plays in our marriages — specifically, the discord it can cause if not properly understood. I am not talking about the behavior but the motivations behind the behavior. I am talking about how we are wired and how that wiring can lead even the best of spouses grappling with wrong conclusions. The tool that I use to assist couples in understanding this extremely important foundational contributor to marital strife is the Myers-Briggs Type Indicator. There are, of course, others. Some people are familiar with DISC, The Big Five, or others that do pretty much the same thing.

The point is not to extol the virtues of the MBTI but to illustrate how important it is to know and understand the personality-driven behaviors and why they take place. This is most important with behaviors that our spouse engages in that we, simply put, do not like. My preference is to use the MBTI. It is the most widely-used personality inventory in the world. Many of the Fortune 500 companies (80% of them, according to CNBC) to this day find use with the MBTI. The instrument is based on the work of psychiatrist Carl Jung. Jung posited that personality manifests itself via specific types that all people possess. However, these traits manifest themselves in differing combinations leading to differing ways of processing information, making decisions, and organizing the world. We have neither the time nor the inclination here to go into detail regarding every one of the 16 personality types espoused by the MBTI, but we do need to understand the influence personality has on marital relationships.

As I said, I have used the MBTI since the beginning to help couples better understand the "why" of their spouse's behavior. It is not only one of the most valuable tools I have at my disposal; it is also one of the most popular parts of the marriage seminar. Virtually every single couple (including those initially skeptical) finds a tremendous amount of value in this endeavor. But this discussion is not about recommending the MBTI or to suggest that you have to take it or any other personality instrument. The point of this discussion is to convince you how personality (and its associated behaviors) can contribute to tremendous marital discord if we don't understand why it is happening. Asking "why" is the pertinent question. Understanding that is not 50% of the battle — it's more like 90%. I have a theory as to why this is so. For me, understanding the role personality plays in marital distress just articulates in a practical and understandable way what we already inherently suspect about ourselves. I liken the benefit of understanding my spouse's personality motives to a line from the famous novel, *To Kill a Mockingbird*.

In that seminal book, Atticus Finch advises his daughter, Scout, saying, "You never really understand a person until you climb into his skin and walk around in it." Notice Atticus eschews the traditional rendering of the truism by suggesting walking in someone else's skin, as opposed to the more well-known idea of walking in another's shoes. The obvious question is then: how do we put ourselves into someone else's skin? Understanding what motivates my spouse's actions allows me the opportunity to see what it is like in someone else's skin. It forces me to consider how someone else thinks, makes decisions, and how they view the world. On my own, I cannot do this. It is not in our nature to do this.

We are all egocentric beings by nature. We think that all people think like us — and if they don't, they should. Our natural state does not lend itself to walking in someone else's skin. Personality instruments provide a pathway to doing so. It is to provide a possible explanation for behavior that doesn't involve us leaping to the lowest common denominator — that is, that my spouse is engaging in this behavior on purpose to annoy or anger me.

In fact, to make this point, I always draw attention to the three fatal mistakes people make concerning the MBTI (and other instruments), especially as it relates to the marital relationship. The first mistake is to treat the MBTI as a panacea. The MBTI does not explain everything about behavior or personality. There is nothing out there that does that. The developers of the MBTI never claimed that it explains everything about personality. While it does not explain everything (people are much too complicated for that), it does explain a great deal. It is not perfect. But there is an old saying: don't let the perfect be the enemy of the good. The MBTI is good, not perfect. Expecting a perfect explanation via the MBTI is the height of unrealistic expectations.

The second mistake people make is viewing their own MBTI personality type myopically. What do I mean by that? Though we may have a dominant personality trait over and against its opposite on that trait spectrum, that doesn't mean that we have the characteristics of that type *only*. For example, if you are an extrovert (as opposed to an introvert) on the MBTI spectrum, that doesn't mean that you are extroverted at every moment of your life. Extroverts need their introverted moments, and introverts need their extroverted moments. So we all have aspects of every personality type in the spectrum, we just prefer some over others. Some are more dominant than others. But we cannot view our MBTI type in a vacuum.

And lastly, the third biggest mistake people make in understanding their MBTI trait is the tendency to use the results as an excuse for bad behavior. We may be wired a certain way, but that doesn't mean that we are free to ignore the negative aspects that may accompany most personality traits. For example, I am an INTJ. I don't expect that to mean too much to you if you are unfamiliar with the MBTI. Suffice it to say that one of the more undesirable personality quirks associated with many (though

23

certainly not all) INTJs is the tendency to come across as distant and aloof. I am aware of that tendency, but I'll be honest — before I understood this via the MBTI, I was not nearly as aware of it as I was after. I was a chaplain. I am a pastor and teacher. I need to engage people, and I need for them to understand my care for them and my desire to help them. If I simply viewed my aloofness as "well, that's just the way I am," then my aloofness could be hurtful to people. It can communicate disinterest and emotional distance. I don't want that. That is a negative aspect of my personality. I must work to be aware of that and work to overcome it. The MBTI gives me the tool to do that as opposed to providing me with an "out" to not even try. I don't want to use the MBTI to allow my personality to be a liability. I want to use it to help me overcome the negative aspects inherent in all personality types.

Allow me to give you a real world example of how this works and how the MBTI can assist us to do what should be natural to us, and that is to give our spouse the benefit of the doubt. In order to best see the potential effectiveness of understanding the role that inherent personality traits plays in marital relationships, let me share with you how it affected my relationship with my wife.

As stated earlier, from an MBTI perspective, I am an INTJ. The "I" in question here designates the fact that I am an introvert. To be clear, I did not need the MBTI to alert me to the fact that I am an introvert. My earliest recollection of social aspects of my life are rooted in the fact that I have been painfully shy for most of my existence. I certainly was not shocked by the conclusion from taking the MBTI. In fact, when I was in grade school, one of the subjects I constantly got "needs improvement" marks for was "class participation". This illustrates two things. First, that I was (and still am) an introvert. Two, that the culture rewards extraversion.

So you may be saying that I am making an argument against my own position by suggesting the MBTI didn't tell me anything I didn't already know. But not so fast. While the MBTI corroborated the "what" that I already knew, it also introduced me to the "why" of my introversion. And that is something I didn't know. Neither did my wife. I can't tell you how important this is in conjunction with the marital relationship. Virtually all of us can see the "what" in our spouse's behavior. And why not? It is right there in front of us. If my spouse is being unusually quiet, I can see the "what" of that behavior quite readily. I can see them being quiet. I can hear them being quiet. I know they are being quiet. What I don't know is why.

Here is where the MBTI can allow us to get into our spouse's skin and walk around a bit. Because I don't know if you've noticed this or not, but human beings are peculiar creatures. If we see a behavior from our spouse (or any person for that matter) that we don't like, but we don't know why the spouse is acting like this, we perceive a gap in the information. Right? I mean, I can see the behavior. I don't like the behavior. But I don't know why it is taking place. This means I have some information but not all of it. There is a gap in the information. And we don't like gaps. Especially when they involve someone important to us. So instead of engaging in helpful activities to determine the reason, we will more than likely fill in the gap ourselves. And we will do so, more times than not, with the worst possible scenario.

For example, my wife is out by herself, and the last thing she told me was that she would be home by 6 pm. It is now 9 pm, and she's not home. She has not called to let me know she was going to be late. She is not answering her phone when I call. And it's a perfectly good phone, by the way. She is not at a family member's house, because I've called. Now I have no problem seeing the behavior, and it is behavior I don't like. She is three hours late, she has not called, she is not answering her phone, and she is not at a family member's house. I can see the "what" — it is the behavior I don't like. But there is a gap in the information. I don't know why this behavior is taking place. So I will fill in the gap.

Therefore, since I have all of this information, and I am going to come to a conclusion (i.e. fill in the gap), what is the first thing I am going to think about this situation? I have used this scenario many times in my marriage seminars. I have given the participants the option to say out loud what my conclusion is going to be. The results are predictable. The only logical conclusion is that my wife is dead on the side of the road. It has to be the answer. When I let the participants yell out possible conclusions, I get things like "she was in an accident," "she got lost," "she is having an affair." Do you know how long I have to let these answers go on before I get one that doesn't involve something bad? Quite a while. In all of the years that I have used this example, I have had only one person start out by saying, "maybe she lost track of time and her phone died." One person, in 20 years of retreats, defaulted to that answer. Everyone else went to a worst-case scenario. Because that is what we do when we have a gap in the information. And the closer we are to the person personally and emotionally, the more likely we are to select the worst case scenario.

Herein lies the simple brilliance of the MBTI. It allows and encourages me to fill in the gaps with something much more rational and reasonable when I see behavior in my spouse that I don't like and don't understand. This was especially the case with my introversion. People think being an introvert simply means being shy. When I ask the group to tell me about introverts, I get answers like "shy," "keeps to themselves," "quiet," "withdrawn." While those are true, those are behaviors. Again, we focus on the behaviors rather than the reason behind the behaviors. Once I

26

understood what the MBTI could tell me about the "why" of behaviors, it changed everything for me.

Being a chaplain is an extroverted job. When I served, I spent virtually my entire day engaging other people. I engaged them socially. I engaged them professionally. I engaged them as a counselor. I engaged them as a friend. I engaged them as a subordinate. I engaged them as a superior. In other words, I engaged people in just about every way imaginable. One of the foundational elements of the MBTI, as it relates to introversion, is that it is more than behavior. This paradigm points out that introverts, in fact, are introverted because that is where they draw their energy from. Introverts are energized by being by themselves. Extroverts, on the other hand, are energized by being around people and engaging them. In contrast, introverts are physically, socially, and emotionally drained by engaging other people for prolonged periods.

If being around people was draining, then only by being alone could I be recharged. So what does this have to do with my relationship with my wife? After spending all day engaging with people, I would then go home to a house full of other people. My family. They missed me. They were waiting anxiously for me to get home. They wanted to spend time with me. And I wanted to spend time with them. However, I was completely spent. I had engaged with people all day, and my battery was running on empty. I had this routine I would engage in once I got home. I would come in, say hello to everyone, engage my wife for a moment, and then I would go into our bedroom and do nothing. I would just sit quietly for a bit. But there was a problem.

My wife would see my behavior. And after spending all day at work away from my family, she wasn't particularly fond of the fact that, once I finally got home, I would immediately disappear for a bit. So let's apply what we talked about just a few minutes ago. My wife sees my behavior. She doesn't like it. She sees the "what," but she doesn't know the "why." In other words, there is a gap in the information. And what do we do with the gaps? We fill them with the worst possible scenario. Therefore, what could she conclude? She could conclude, "he doesn't want to be home," "he is angry with me," "he is angry with the kids," "he would rather be back at work," "he doesn't love us." By the way, none of those things would have been true. But you can see how those conclusions might have been reached and what impact they were going to have on the relationship.

My bride came to know the reason for my behavior. She knows I am an introvert, and I was embedded in an extroverted job. She knew that it was an emotionally, socially, and physically draining situation. She then came to know that I *needed* that few minutes alone, not that I *wanted* to be away from my family. And she knew that, if she gave me this time, I was a much more attentive husband and father for the rest of the evening. Because now she understood the "why," and it wasn't any of the "whys" she thought to be true. Here's the catch: she didn't know this in year one or two or even year five of our marriage. She came to see this because of the insight provided by the truth behind the MBTI. And this is just a small example of this amazing tool's effectiveness.

Personality, the way we are wired, plays a huge role in marital strife. It does. There are behaviors we do not like in our spouses, mostly because we do not know why they take place. Some are intentional and need to be dealt with. That much is true. But many of them are simply a product of the quirks inherent in all personality types. The MBTI helps me to do what should (but most times does not) come naturally, and that is to give the benefit of the doubt to the one person I love most in the world.

Moving on.

All of this to say, this has not been an endeavor to promote the MBTI (or any other instrument, for that matter). I hope that is not the takeaway here. I think it's helpful, but it's only helpful from the standpoint that it gives us a passageway to doing what this section is really suggesting: find out how your spouse is wired. Take the time to do so to enable you to give them the benefit of the doubt when it comes to certain behaviors. To be clear, I'm not talking about obviously bad behavior. If your spouse is committing adultery, we don't need to see the role that personality plays and conclude, "he's just wired that way." We don't need to endure physical abuse because maybe we've concluded, "he's just wired that way."

I will address this in more detail later in the section entitled "Relationship Killers," but, for now, let me tell you something. In my experience, the vast majority of causes related to marital discord have nothing to do with what I call the "Big Three". The Big Three are adultery, physical abuse, and substance abuse. To be honest, when I had a couple that was experiencing those, there was a pretty straight-forward course of action that could be delineated. No, the vast majority (and I mean *vast*) of marital discord is directly related to one spouse (or both) simply not understanding behaviors that, on the surface, might seem fairly innocuous. And that is because they are focusing on the behavior, rather than what is driving the behavior. And once you understand the behavior and realize that the behavior is simply a quirk of the person you love most in the world, then it makes it amazingly easy to give each other the benefit of the doubt over behaviors that we do not like. The MBTI does that for me, which is why I mention it. There are plenty of free, online, scaled-down versions of many personality inventories that can help with this. The point is: we need help with this. I cannot tell you how important it is that we really know why our spouses do what they do, however we can do that. It is essential that we know because it does not come to us naturally to know.

There are so many other foundational issues we could cover in this introduction, but I really want you to get to the meat of the book. I don't want to bog you down in the introduction to the detriment of what lay ahead. I just wanted to touch base on a few things that, if we do not get right from the beginning, we will get wrong at the conclusion. That's why I wanted to make sure we had our presuppositions correctly aligned before we move forward. Even a putt that is slightly off at the point of impact will end up being way off once it gets near the hole. I don't want you to be way off when we get to the end. Some of the other elements I left out of this introduction will be introduced elsewhere in the book. I will also expand on some of the topics mentioned here as we move forward.

I also don't want this book to be a call to "do more" or "be better". You will not find a list of things you have to do in order to be a better husband or wife. Think of the Marriage Pyramid as a gauge to determine where you are in your marriage and the obstacles that may be in place to keep you from getting there. That's the whole idea behind it. In a weird kind of way it is a bit like the pain scale used when seeing a doctor. You know how that works. The doctor or nurse involved will ask if you have any pain and how intense the pain is. To get perspective, they determine this by giving you a scale of 1-10 with 1 being no pain and 10 being the worst. The Marriage Pyramid does the same thing. It is tool to measure where you are in your marriage and, more importantly, where you want to be. The Marriage Pyramid is not a method to follow as much as it is a barometer of our marital reality. And it is there to reveal to us what is keeping us from having the marriage God wants for us. Nothing more, nothing less.

But I think we've spent enough time here. Let's get to the good stuff, shall we?

Chapter Two
Love

Before we get into the nuts and bolts of what role love plays in the marital relationship and why we need to have a discussion on something that must be painfully obvious, let me take a few moments to shed some light onto the evolution of the Marriage Pyramid. As I stated earlier, the foundational elements of this paradigm began to manifest themselves during my initial duty station while I served as a Navy Chaplain. Back in about 1998, I was tasked with participating in a marital/premarital program the Navy and the Marine Corps used to help ensure healthy marriages in the Sea Services.

Even at that time, divorce was a huge problem within the military, and the effect it had on morale and readiness was palpable. In fact, in 1993, General Carl Mundy, then Commandant of the Marine Corps, enacted a controversial (and ultimately unsuccessful) edict designed to force the Marine Corps to cease recruiting potential Marines who happened to be married and to enforce a rule that stated first-tour Marines could not get married. The outcry from the civilian political leadership was predictable. And the edict did not last long before General Mundy rescinded the policy.

On the surface, it probably wasn't the best idea. However, General Mundy's perception of the problems regarding military service and marriage was spot-on. It wasn't that a married Marine couldn't do her or his job; it's that, too many times, these marriages involved turmoil that led to divorce, which strained nerves and resources. General Mundy was just too pragmatic for his own good. The problem of marital dysfunction in the military was real. His solution was seen by many as a bit… much.

Therefore, what happened was a renewed approach to marriage within the Sea Services that focused on education and training. At the Marine Air-Ground Combat Center in Twentynine Palms, California, if you were a Sailor or Marine that wanted to get married, you had to attend a three-day seminar entitled PREP. That was my introduction into participating in marriage seminars and my first opportunity to put into practice some of my marriage philosophies.

I was trained in PREP and found a good bit of it helpful. However, I also knew the difficulties the newly married couples were going to face and saw a significant gap in the material they were being taught. So I thought about how to best incorporate my ideas into the sections of PREP I normally taught. And the Marriage Pyramid was born. Not as it is in today's iteration, but rather an infant of an idea that has grown and matured over the years. As I stated earlier, it has not changed dramatically. I don't think really good ideas should change too dramatically, or they weren't that good of an idea in the first place. But it has matured and grown into the model we have today.

Oh, I messed around with a variety of shapes. I used a spiral once. I experimented with Venn diagrams. But just as Walt Disney was fond of saying that "it all started with a mouse," I can easily say that the Marriage Pyramid all started with a shape. Only it wasn't as much the shape that intrigued me as the reason for it and the idea behind it developed by an extraordinary mind. The mind belonged to Dr. Abraham Maslow, and the idea behind it was his Hierarchy of Needs.

Let me be clear, I am not an expert on Maslow nor do I ascribe to the totality of his varied fields of study. I really do not know much about him outside of the ideas prescribed in this theory of human psychological development. I was in a high school psychology class when I was first introduced to his now-famous and elegantly simple theory on how psychologically healthy people develop and why so many fail to do so. Again, do not mistake my admiration for his model as an endorsement of everything he postulated. What I was drawn to was its logic and simplicity.

The idea suggested by Maslow was that, if a human being were to develop to his or her optimal psychological health (a position he termed self-actualization), other more increasingly necessary rudimentary building blocks must be in place. Again, the form and structure and idea behind the model was way more impactful on me than the intricacies of the theory. His use of the triangle to illustrate this point was perfect. In order to have the best life one could hope for, there had to be foundational elements present that would inevitably lead to that life. And if any of these building blocks were missing, then the optimal life could not be reached.

That is, in part, why he used the pyramid to represent his idea. The goal is to be at the top of the pyramid. However, if any of the steps below the top one were missing, then one could NOT get to the top. The simple elegance of this idea played a huge role in my desire to use the same type of idea when it comes to marriage. Think of it this way: the top step in the Marriage Pyramid represents the optimal marriage possible for that couple. Not the perfect marriage, which does not exist. It also does not represent the fact that the optimal marriage will look exactly the same for every single couple. There are way too many personal variables to come up with one single picture of a perfect marriage. But there is an optimal marriage possible for every single couple.

However, there are also foundational steps below the top one that must be present or the optimal marriage *is not possible*. Notice I didn't say that without these foundational steps an optimal marriage would not be *likely*. I said it would not be possible. That's the whole idea behind the Marriage Pyramid. I have counseled hundreds and hundreds of married couples, and the vast number of these have just affirmed the ideas I had about marriage via the Marriage Pyramid. Every couple that gets married places their eyes at the top of the Marriage Pyramid, even if they've never seen it. They want the optimal marriage. They do not want to get divorced. However, they never see or understand that, in order to get to the top step in the Pyramid, the other steps must be in place.

That's why we are going to start off with basics and move to the more advanced levels. We are going to make our way through the Pyramid and talk about what each step represents and how important they are, especially as they are related to the Biblical view of marriage and the ideal that God has for this amazing institution. I just wanted to take a moment to give credit where it was due to Dr. Maslow and his amazing triangle that got me thinking about what that might mean in marriage.

Love.

I already know what you're thinking: do we really have to talk about how important love is to the marital relationship? Isn't that akin to shocking truths such as, the sun is hot and water is wet? In a way, yes. But that presupposes a very important point that we have to consider in order to come to that conclusion. The presupposition is this: I know what the definition of "love" is. May I suggest that, for the vast majority of us, we absolutely do *not* know the most accurate definition of love. Not the definition that is related to God's Word and His perspective of love. Oh, we have a definition of it, but does it line up with the reality of this construct as defined by the Creator? I'm not so sure. We know the world's definition of love. How the world portrays it in books, poetry, songs, movies, and television shows. But is that the working definition we should be using?

In order to best understand this in the proper way, let's take a look at what God's Word has to say regarding the philosophy of the world. Did you know that the word "philosophy" is used just once in the entire Bible? It is used in Colossians 2:8. We will look at this passage in much more detail in just a minute, but suffice it to say that the Bible warns us about putting our faith in the philosophy of the world. This is most germane to our discussion about love, because the world has a philosophy about love that inundates us at every turn. To be able to see the fallacy in the world's version of love and how it has poisoned our understanding of it, we have to see the root causes of errant, worldly philosophy in the first place.

The reason I believe this passage is included in the Bible is that God (of course) knew the human penchant of placing very smart people (or people that seem to be smart) on a pedestal. We have seen this with scientists, philosophers, and entrepreneurs galore throughout the history of the world. Not too long ago (related to the writing of this book), the brilliant physicist, Stephen Hawking, released a book coming to the conclusion that there was no God. Immediately, secularists representing the world's way of thinking glommed on to this to somehow suggest that the debate was over, the brilliant Stephen Hawking had spoken, and so this just confirms that there is no God.

What I couldn't understand is that no one really ever asked the all-important question. The question is this: has Stephen Hawking ever been wrong about anything? I mean anything? Has he ever made a mistake? Of course, the answers to these questions are painfully obvious. Stephen Hawking has been wrong about a lot of things. Because he's human. He has even been wrong about ideas and hypotheses within his field of expertise. If he has been wrong a lot, then why couldn't he be wrong about there being no God? Not only *could* he be wrong, he *is*. But our penchant to view very intelligent people as nearly infallible is the reason God warns us about the world's philosophy. And since our threshold for intelligence-valuing has hit rock-bottom (with athletes, actors, and musicians routinely labeled as brilliant), it is more important than ever that we get this right when it comes to love.

We readily embrace the world's definition and view of love to the detriment of God's definition. We hold on to an errant definition of love, which leads to definitively unrealistic expectations of what that love looks like in the context of marriage. So yes, we need to start with a proper understanding of love by first comparing the world's philosophy to God's truth.

Colossians 2:8

Since this is a book on marriage and not on Biblical hermeneutics, I will keep this brief. But if we are to understand this foundational element of marriage (love) and we agree that the world provides us with an errant view of this element, then we must also understand the differences between the world's philosophies and God's truth. Fortunately, though this is seen throughout Scripture, we have a passage that succinctly describes these differences. Therefore, let's take a few minutes to examine how the world differs in its approach to "truth" at the expense of the actual truth posited by God in His Word.

Again, it is worth noting that this passage contains the only use of the word "philosophy" in all of Scripture. And, without rehashing my earlier assertion to the point of mere repetition, it is important to remember what gravitas we have traditionally placed on philosophers throughout history. From Aristotle and Plato, to Christian philosophers such as Augustine and Aquinas. Some of these names have been spoken with reverence for more than 2,000 years. There are, of course, other names too numerous to mention, leading up to this very day. Bright, insightful minds trying their best to convince us of truth that may or may not be. But for the secular philosopher, what is their foundation? Upon what do they build their worldly philosophies? God was gracious enough to give us this answer to enlighten and warn us.

When Paul wrote his letter to the churches in Colossae, it is believed that he had not yet visited this area personally (Col. 2:1). Because they had not had the advantage of hearing Paul's teaching in person, Paul was very interested in making sure they understood more of the basic ideas related to Christianity, in order for them to continue to grow in their faith. It doesn't take a PhD in theology to determine what many of the issues these churches faced by reading Paul's epistles. If he is addressing a particular subject, then it is a safe bet that he does so because that particular church (or conglomeration of churches in that area) was struggling in that subject. Since Paul warns the Colossians of the philosophical underpinnings of the world, then it stands to reason they were struggling with this a bit in their church. And what did Paul warn them about?

"See to it that no one takes you captive by philosophy and empty deceit, according to human tradition, according to the elemental spirits of the world, and not according to Christ" (Col. 2:8, ESV). Notice immediately how Paul (under the inspiration of the Holy Spirit) lays the groundwork for us understanding how dangerous the world's philosophy ultimately is. He does not simply dismiss it as a difference of opinion or a plethora of maxims that although wrong are, for the most part, harmless. He begins immediately by stating that adhering to and embracing the world's philosophy is tantamount to being in captivity.

Also note that Paul does not differentiate as to what kinds of worldly philosophy we are to avoid. He does not suggest that Aristotelian philosophy is somehow a bit better than Platonic philosophy because it influenced Augustine and was interwoven into his theology. There is nothing in this passage that suggests in any way, shape, or form that any worldly philosophy is "okay" or that some might be better than others. This idea is corroborated throughout Scripture, as well. Jesus warns us that the world will hate us because it first hated Him (John 15:18-25). Paul, in his extraordinary treatise to the church in Rome, states clearly that we are not to "be conformed to this world, but be transformed by the renewing of your mind" (Romans 12:2a). Solomon warns us in his book of maxims that "there is a way that seems right to a man, but its end is the way to death" (Proverbs 14:12, ESV).

The message is clear throughout Scripture, and specifically here in Colossians, that the world's philosophies, as rooted in the errant presuppositions espoused in the passage, are completely wrong. And not only are they wrong, they are dangerous to the Believer. That doesn't mean that every once in a while the world doesn't "accidentally" get something right. But when they do, it is because they are merely affirming what Scripture has already said clearly and eloquently, whether they give credit to God or not. This was seen some years ago when an organization spent, no doubt, probably thousands of dollars on a study that examined the causes of workplace burn-out. Their conclusion? That people were working too many days without rest and that, to better optimize efficiency, human beings really did not need to work seven days a week. In fact, the study concluded that people were much more efficient if they had at least one day off a week in which to recharge.

The study originators hailed this as breaking news. However, they would have saved themselves a lot of money and time if they had checked to see that God gave them this information about 5,000 years ago. The world can sometimes get it "right," but only when they confirm what God has already said. But human philosophy doesn't work that way. The main reason it doesn't is because of sin.

The one refrain you will hear from me, because it is continuously echoed throughout the Bible, is that sin corrupts everything it touches. And it touches everything, especially our mind and heart (Matt. 5:28). Since that is the case, any worldly or cultural "truth" we devise on our own is also tainted by sin and therefore untrustworthy. This is what Paul is warning us about in Colossians and why this entire conversation is apropos to a discussion about the true meaning of love and its role in the marital relationship.

Remember, the world consistently and continuously bombards us with its philosophy regarding love: what it is, what it is not, and how we can recognize it. However, worldly philosophy is tainted by sin and, by definition, has to be incorrect unless it accidentally stumbles into supporting a scriptural understanding of love. Get it? Hence the reason for Paul's warning and his simple but clear definition of all worldly philosophy. Let's take a closer look.

Paul gives us the three criteria from which all worldly philosophy flows. The three criteria are as follows: 1) it is "according to human tradition;" 2) it is "according to the elemental spirits of the world;" 3) it is "not according to Christ" (Col. 2:8). Now we could write an entire book (a rather large one, in fact) on the details of these three criteria and what they have meant to the world and to Christianity. But as I stated earlier, that is not the focus of this book. I merely want to build the foundation for why we should identify and reject the world's view of love in order for our marriage to be the best in Christ that it can be.

For our purposes, however, the takeaway here is that the world's view of love (with which we have been inundated virtually every second of our lives) is untrustworthy, ultimately because of sin and the fact that it is not rooted in Christ. Again, remember Paul's warning to the Colossians (and consequently, to us). Paul exhorts us to not become "captive" to these false pronouncements from the world. It is interesting to note the nuances of the phrase "captive" in the original Koine Greek.

In the original language, the term "captive" comes from a word that literally means "to lead off as prey, carry off as booty, rob, or kidnap" (Zhodiates, pg. 1324). The word carries the sense that captives are stalked by those who see them as prey for the express purpose of robbing them of something. This word was used, no doubt, to convey the idea that this is exactly what sin desires to do to a person. We know this from what reporters would call "a very reliable source."

After the Fall, things began to unravel pretty quickly for humanity. Adam and Eve's disobedience ushered sin into all of humanity from that time onward, and it didn't take but one generation for that sin to manifest itself in the ultimate way, with the recording of the first murder. This familiar story is well-known, but perhaps God's warning prior to the act is not so well-known. After God rejects Cain's sacrifice, the Scripture reports that Cain "was very angry, and his face fell" (Genesis 4:5b, ESV). God did not leave Cain to stew in his anger but actually tried to help him. He warned Cain about sin and made this extremely important declaration that not only should Cain have heeded, but so should we all: "Sin is crouching at the door. Its desire is for you, but you must rule over it" (Genesis 4:7b, ESV).

Remember, Paul warned us not to be taken captive by the philosophy of the world. And here in Genesis, we see why. Because it is the desire of sin to take us captive in order to rule over us. That is the nature of the Adversary and his tool, sin. Paul knew that sin desires to control every aspect of our lives. Our heart. Our mind. Our actions. Our marriage. That's why we're talking about all of this sin stuff in the first place. As Believers, we have a tendency to allow the things of the world to creep into the parts of our life that are supposed to be influenced by God and His truth. These worldly ideas and philosophies are generated by sinful minds at enmity with God's truth. God said through Isaiah that "my thoughts are not your thoughts, neither are your ways my ways, declares the Lord" (Isaiah 55:8, ESV).

This is, of course, 100% correct about everything, including the world's view of love and its relationship as the foundational building block for the Marriage Pyramid. We must get this right. It is of paramount importance. If we do not, then everything we build on the subsequently shaky foundation will not stand. The world has told us what love is, what it is not, and how it should be applied. And they are wrong. They cannot help but be wrong because their view is tainted with sin that leaves everyone blind to the truth of God (2 Cor. 4:4). So as we move forward in our discussion of the foundational level of the Marriage Pyramid (love), let's do so with a desire to see this amazing construct in the Light in which it was intended to be seen, through the prism of God's Word.

What's love got to do with it?

As I have stated, there is a universe of difference between what the culture defines as love and what God defines as love. And I will go a bit further here. I do not believe it is possible for any human being to truly love another person without first having experienced God's love. I say that unapologetically. Oh, the world can give you an imitation of love, a sort of form of love, but it will not be love in the manner in which we were created to experience it. Which is why we cannot embrace the world's view of love as the foundational element for marriage. It *will not* be this way because it *cannot* be this way. Remember, I claimed clearly and without ambiguity that I would look at all aspects of this subject through the prism of God's Word. That is my beginning and my ending point. With that in mind, I give you one of many passages dealing with love from a God perspective: "The one who does not love does not know God, for God is love" (1 John 4:8 NASB). Again, this is not a book on hermeneutics, so we will keep this as brief as is prudent, so as not to get bogged down. But we must get this right.

Let's look at the last part of the verse and the interesting verbiage used in God's Word. It does not say that God created love or imparts love or manufactures it from time to time. The verse states that God IS love. He is the personification of love. He is the well from which love must be drawn. Apart from God, we cannot love. At least, we cannot love in the manner in which God designed. In Jesus' last hours with His disciples, prior to His arrest and crucifixion, He shared a final meal with them and imparted amazing and comforting truths. One of the last statements He made during this time is recorded in the last part of John Chapter 17. Remember, in context, Jesus here is not only speaking to His disciples but to all of "those who *will* [italics mine] believe in Me" (John 17:20b NKJV). So he is talking to me and to you, if you are a Believer. Later in the chapter, Jesus makes the following statement as He is praying to the Father for the disciples and future Believers: "I have declared to them Your name, and will declare it,

43

that the love with which You loved me may be in them [bolding mine], and I in them" (John 17:26 NKJV).

I know we are taking these verses out of context but, for the sake of time, it is necessary. I implore you to seek out any and all verses I use to see for yourselves whether they mean what I am claiming they do. I find the verbiage again very interesting here. Jesus is praying that the love of God the Father, specifically the love He has for the Son, be IN Believers. Why would Jesus use this verbiage? As Occam's razor reminds us, the simplest answer is usually the correct one. And the simplest answer to this question is that, if Jesus is praying for the love of God to be IN Believers, then that means that, without God, that love is not already there. See, here is where the culture lies to us. The Bible states that God is love, the world will tell you that love is God. The world will tell you that its version of love... a thing that we can't define, don't know what causes it, seems to come and go with the wind, and actually motivates some people to violence is, in fact, god. The world states very clearly that we do not need God in order to experience, feel, and give love. But without the very source of love, how can anyone understand or engage love?

Love becomes whatever you want it to be or, more often, what you don't want it to be. It becomes circumstantial, petty, easily lost by those who displease us, and just as easily given to another who does please us, at least for the moment. Probably the best explanation I have heard of the difference between God's love (the only true love) and the world's love (a cheap imitation, at best) was provided by the great Reformer, Martin Luther. In a nutshell, Luther stated that all human love is motivated by selfishness, in some way or another. We love a type of food because of the way it tastes to us. We love a certain sports team because of the thrill of victory *we* get when *they* accomplish greatness. We love people because of what they mean to us or what they do for us. We love

44

them because they are beautiful or dutiful or they say the right things at the right time or they take care of us. The common denominator in the world's love is always ourselves.

God's amazing love is the exact opposite. He does not love us (by "us," I mean Believers) because of any inherent value we have in any way, shape, or form. He does not love us because we are smart (1 Corinthians 3:19). He does not love us because we are "good" (Romans 3:10; Mark 10:18). He does not love us because we love Him (Romans 3:11). He does not love us because we have a good heart (Jeremiah 17:9). He does not love us because we do good things (Isaiah 64:6). He does not love us because of any of those things. He loves us *despite* these things. His love is completely unconditional and undeserved. Yet He loves us anyway. He loves us despite the fact that, if we came across such creatures as ourselves, we would deem then as unlovable. That, my friends, is God's love. The only true love. In ourselves, we cannot generate this type of love. That's why Jesus asked that God the Father put this love into us from the outside. If we could generate this love ourselves, then Jesus would have told us to try harder, work more, exercise to get this love to a proper level. But He knew that would be the height of folly because the love has to be in us in the first place. And, without God, this is not possible. God *is* love, and only He can dispense love — the kind of love that tells us to love our enemies and to pray for those who persecute us (Matthew 5:44).

So we need to understand that, while love is the foundational element that leads to an amazing marriage, we absolutely must have access to the source of all love in order to truly love our spouses. And the world's cheap imitation of love does not give us the opportunity to love our spouse as we need to, in order to have the optimal marriage. Why? Because the world devalues and deconstructs love down to the lowest common denominator. The world cheapens it and then packages it so that it seems valuable.

And it does so by perpetuating the single biggest hoax related to love that has led millions of people to divorce court and many others to a loveless marriage. And it all starts with a feeling.

More than a feeling?

When I present this material in my marriage seminars, it is often suggested that I am trying to suck all of the fun out of love. That is not precisely true, but some of you will think I'm giving it a good try. This, of course, is not my intent, but I do want us to be able to get a good handle on what love is and, almost as importantly, what it is not. As I mentioned in the previous section, I maintain that it is impossible to love anyone (especially your spouse) without having a personal, intimate relationship with God through His Son, Jesus Christ. That doesn't mean that people who are not Believers cannot express some type of love to others. It simply means that it will only be a weak facsimile of the love God wants us to enjoy. If God is love (and He is) and you do not have a relationship with God, then it stands to reason that you will not be able to tap into that reservoir of love that emanates from God.

It is vitally important to our paradigm that we properly understand what love is, if we exist under the assumption that love is the foundational element of a marriage relationship. In that vein, let's now examine a bit more closely the errant philosophy that the world upholds regarding the ultimate human personal relationship on the planet: the relationship between a husband and a wife.

I never watched the JJ Abrams television show, *Lost*, as it originally aired. It aired on ABC for six seasons between 2004 and 2010. However, like many folks, I did catch up with it once it hit Netflix. Actually, my wife and kids started watching it to begin with and constantly raved about the show. After a while, I became too curious to hold out any longer, and I joined in as well. There was a great deal I liked about the show. The stories (for the most part) were interesting, and the characters were (for the most part) compelling. For the record, I was a huge fan of Mr. Echo. For those of you who are purveyors of the show, you know that the stories were sometimes very convoluted and non-linear. Sometimes it made sense, sometimes not so much. There were also a large number of subplots, due to the sizable cast. It's one of the things I enjoyed about the show. One subplot in particular is very germane to this discussion, and it concerns the main female protagonist, Kate Austen.

Without getting too much into the weeds, there was a background story related to Kate in which she was on the run from the law after killing her mother's abusive husband. This guy was not Kate's biological father, and she had watched her mother be systematically abused for years at the hands of this terrible man. She rigged an explosion to look like an accident and, afterwards, made the mistake of telling her mother, convinced her mother would side with Kate. She misjudged — badly. Kate's mother informed the police about the murder perpetrated by her daughter, which sent Kate on the run. The inevitable confrontation with her mother was teased for seasons on the show, until it eventually happened.

Kate finally got the opportunity to confront her mother and try to understand why she would choose an alcoholic, abusive husband over her own flesh and blood. The answer she received from her mother is representative of the idea that too many people have about love and why it constantly eludes them. When Kate asked that all-important question as to why her own mother would side with an abusive husband, her mother responded, "You can't help who you love." I am 53 years old. I think I have gotten to the place in my life where I can honestly say that I have a certain amount of wisdom. Wisdom is different than knowledge. There is a large number of extremely smart people who have the wisdom of a mentally defective woodchuck (for all of you woodchuck lovers out there, I apologize). Age helps with wisdom, but it's no guarantee. I have seen plenty of older folks who have lived a rich, full life with a myriad of experiences and still have little to no wisdom at all. I have seen younger folks with not nearly that many life experiences who have a great deal of wisdom. I have seen a lot, experienced a lot, learned a lot, and been educated a lot. And that statement made by Kate's mother is one of the single most idiotic statements I have ever heard a human being utter.

Before you say, "Hey, those words were put there by a writer in a fictional show," let me tell you something: I have heard that statement, and others congruous with that one, from hundreds of people I have counseled over that past 20 years. I have seen that very same message preached from the prophets of the secular via their mediums in television, movies, and songs. That errant view of love has even made it into our vernacular on the subject. How many times have you heard, or even said, something about *"falling in love?"* I was an English major in college — I came to the conclusion a long time ago that words mean things. They are not just throwaway platitudes. There is something much deeper related to the words we speak, and that is extremely true with the phrase "I fell in love."

Just look at the verbiage here for a second. The phrase seems to imply that it really has nothing to do with us. That it's not really our fault. I fell in love just as I fell in that hole that I didn't see the other day. I was just walking along, minding my own business and... bam! I fell into a hole, and then I fell in love. Neither of these things were my fault, it just happened. After all, you can't help who you love. Oh, and by the way, if I fell in love with this person, and I couldn't help it, then it's not my fault if I fall out of love, right? See the problem here? We do not take responsibility for our love. It just happens. Nobody's fault. Then I fall in love with someone else, nobody's fault. Want to see a perfect example of this lunacy? Watch Meg Ryan's character in *Sleepless in Seattle*. You can see what this does to love. It relegates it to a construct that is based almost exclusively on feelings. The single biggest mistake all people can make with love in the marriage relationship (Believers do this as well, all the time) is to deconstruct love so that it exists simply as a feeling.

Are there feelings associated with love? Yes! There are wonderful, amazing, extraordinary, nothing-else-like-it feelings associated with being in love. It is the single most intimate relationship we can have with another human being. And the feelings are incredible. We all like those feelings and, in fact, long for those feelings. We will join 50 different dating sites just so we can experience those feelings. But while we are taking a moment to laud the feelings associated with love, let me ask you a very important question: what happens when those feelings are not there? What happens when they wane? What happens when your spouse does something that makes you angry, disappointed, and frustrated? Do you *feel* love then? When you are in the midst of a huge argument with your spouse (which WILL happen), how are those tingly love feelings working out then? Oh, you've got tingly feelings at that point, alright. They just have more to do with rage than love.

In my years of counseling, I have heard some tragically stupid things. And some of the lines I have heard more than any others are: "I'm not in love with him anymore;" "I fell out of love with her;" "I fell in love with someone else." See the mentality behind those statements? The statements are constructed almost as if to suggest that their newfound lack of love for their spouse is not their fault. It is no more their fault then falling into that hole last week. Oh well, what are you gonna do?

People have asked me from time to time to name what I think is the number one reason people get divorced, as it relates to the marriages that I have seen that did not make it. I do not hesitate with my answer. They think I will say infidelity or substance abuse or physical abuse. In my experience, those are not the reasons the vast majority of people get divorced. The number one reason I have seen, time and time again, is this: unrealistic expectations. One or both members of the couple come into that marriage with an expectation of what marriage is supposed to be that is as closely linked to reality as a raven is to a writing desk (my thanks to Lewis Carroll). I remember one Marine coming into my office prior to his getting married to get some advice. He was 18 years old and was getting ready to marry another 18-year-old. I tried my best to talk him out of it — no dice. Having failed at that, we talked about being married.

He offered this interesting statement to me. He said, "I have one goal for my marriage." I was ecstatic. At least he had one goal. That was one goal more than most of the people I counseled. So I asked him what his goal was. He answered, "My goal is to make sure my wife stays happy all the time." I was visibly less ecstatic after that statement. My reply: "Son, you do realize there is a pretty good chance you will mess that up by the end of the evening once you get home, right?" I was not sure what I was most surprised about. The fact that he said that out loud or that he actually believed it? Think about what he said (which, by the way, he probably said many times to his swooning 18-year-old fiancé). He has decided that he himself is going to be personally responsible for another human being's happiness. I told him, as nicely and as plainly as I could, "You will fail." You cannot be responsible for another person's happiness. You can contribute to it, detract from it, but not be responsible for it. The first time he fails at that, his wife will blame him for not completing something that he was powerless to complete. He will first blame himself. Then he will blame her. I'm only human, he'll think. What does she want from me, he'll think. See where I'm going with this?

When love is relegated to only a feeling, the pressure is there to constantly experience that feeling. And feelings/emotions are funny things. They cannot be sustained indefinitely. Have you ever tried to stay angry for 24 hours a day, seven days a week? It's exhausting. You couldn't do it if you tried. Are you happy all the time? Of course not. Why? Because emotions are tied almost exclusively to outside stimuli. I can be the happiest guy in the world, get devastating news, and be the saddest guy in the world in a matter of seconds (read Job). I can be angry or disappointed and get great news, only to have those emotions wane almost as quickly as they began. You absolutely cannot feel an emotion all the time, no matter what that emotion is. That includes love, if you expressly view it as a feeling.

The biggest problem with viewing love as only a feeling is that we are in huge trouble when we don't feel that feeling. Huge trouble. We turn marriage into a performance. If I believe it is my spouse who should make me "feel" love, and I think the only arbiter of love is how I feel, then everything is great so long as my spouse performs. I have lost count of how many couples came into my office on the brink of divorce for no obvious reason, only to tell me that marriage "wasn't what I expected." When I ask them what they expected, I listen to them outline to me what they thought marriage and their spouse would be like. Their expectations were unbelievable. They all related to the idea that their spouse would respond to them exactly as they should all the time. They would never be harsh with them, would do the right things at the right time, and would understand them completely in every instance. I would then ask the following question: "What ever gave you the idea marriage would be like that?"

I would then tell them that, if they were placing an ad in the paper as if this were a job and put those qualifications in there, then no one would take that job. I would also tell them that if they married 1,000 people, they would never find someone to match those expectations.

I love the feelings I have for my bride. But that's not how I know I love her. I love her because I chose to love her. She chose to love me. She didn't "fall" in love with me, because I would be terrified she would "fall" out of love with me. And it would then be nobody's fault. It would just be one of those things. We choose to love our spouses. We absolutely cannot define our love based only on the associated feelings for one huge reason: our spouses will let us down. They will be untruthful at times. They will hurt our feelings. They will sometimes ignore us. They will be grumpy. In other words, they will be human. That's why it is of the utmost importance that we understand the ever-prevalent dangers of treating love exclusively as a feeling. It is not. Because if it is, then when the feeling goes away, so does the love. The world will tell you over and over again that love is a feeling because the world doesn't care whether your marriage survives or not. I do care. That's why I'm telling you the truth. Ravi Zacharias once said, "Love is as much an act of the will as it is an emotion of the heart." Choose to love your broken, sinful spouse. Because we are all broken and sinful, and we all need that love.

I hope I have done some justice to the idea of love and how foundational it is to the marriage relationship. I know this is not breaking news. My goal is not to convince you that love is necessary for the optimal marriage but that cultural misappropriation of love has rendered it unrecognizable within the marriage construct. Love is *not* what the world tells us it is. It is *not* primarily a feelings-based emotion. It is *not* an invented checklist to keep a running tally on how your spouse is not measuring up. God *is* love. And only through Him and His Word are we going to have the proper understanding of love in such a way that we can embrace it as the foundational element of our marriage.

I am convinced that more than half of the marriages in existence in this nation right now do not have a proper, complete, Biblical understanding of what love really is. As such, they do not have the foundational element of the Marriage Pyramid. Therefore, they cannot then move up the very next level of the Pyramid, in hopes of reaching the top. One cannot reach the top of the ladder if one does not have a firm footing on the first rung. I cannot tell you how important it is to get this right. Most people don't. And most people will then languish in a marriage that consistently disappoints them because they have a disappointing understanding of love. You may be one of these people. And I don't want to engage in unnecessary hyperbole, so I won't. You may be one of these people and never get divorced. You may be one of these people and stay married for 30 years. However, you will not have the optimal marriage. Not the one God has for you. And you will not experience the enduring, *sacred* love that the very God of the universe wants you to have. That's why I spent so much time on this absolutely necessary component of the Pyramid. But enough of this — let's move on.

Chapter Three
Safety

Operationalizing constructs.

Getting my PhD was the most academically challenging thing I have ever done in my life. Again, I'm sure this should not be considered breaking news, but I have a point in bringing this up. While there were a lot of things my professors hammered into me over the course of those four years, one of them continues to loom large in my brain. I was constantly told, over and again, that if I was going to examine a construct (whatever that construct might be) and then communicate my findings to others, then I would have to "operationalize my constructs."

I had a general idea of what that advice meant, but I did not appreciate its wisdom until I began to engage in the various research methodologies to examine certain hypotheses. In other words, if I was going to study a construct and engage research methodologies to do so, then I had better be sure that the reader of my work and I would have the same definition of that construct in the first place. Know what I mean?

Take the previous chapter, for example. The foundational element of the Marriage Pyramid is love, correct? But if I don't adequately define and operationalize love, then I can actually encourage the reader to come to a false conclusion. So I can't just use the word "love" — I have to define it for the purposes of this study. Which is what I spent about 20 pages or so doing. I do not want someone to look at the levels of the Marriage Pyramid, see the associated words describing it, and then come to errant conclusions related to a misunderstanding of what those words mean.

For example, someone may never pick up this book but might see a picture of the Marriage Pyramid. They will see the levels: love, safety, growing, becoming one. Then they might say to themselves, "I love my wife. I feel safe with my wife. I grow with my wife. I am one with my wife." They will conclude that they have the optimal marriage and move on, all the while not recognizing that they were applying their own definition to those constructs. Now, to be clear, maybe that person does have the optimal marriage. But that's not the point. We are trying to examine what that means within the context of an operationalized construct. What do I mean when I talk about love or safety or growing or becoming one? It is my job to make sure you understand exactly what I mean when I use those phrases. We have to be on the same sheet of music in that regards, and that burden is on me.

Now, be clear, at the end of all of this you may not agree with my conclusions at all. That is 100% fine. Operationalizing my constructs doesn't mean you will acquiesce to my way of viewing it. It simply means that you will know what I mean when I use these terms. You might disagree with the meaning I came to, but I want more than anything for you to understand what I mean when I use these terms. Can I share an anecdote from my time in the Navy that might illustrate this? I am assuming you said yes.

For those of you who have served in the military, you know that it is an arduous life. One of the more difficult aspects of military life is deploying. Deployments are even more difficult when they involve being placed in harm's way, via a combat zone. For those of you outside of the military, I do not expect you to understand. I know you can sympathize, but you can't understand.

Not unless you've been there and done that. Of all of the difficult things I took part in during my two decades in the Navy, deploying was the most difficult.

Depending on your branch of service, deployments can last anywhere from a few months to a year and a half. Think about that. Think about having to go to your family, look them in the eye, and tell them you were leaving them for a half a year, a year, or a year and a half. It was always devastating leaving my family. We sort of got used to deployments, but we never got good at them. That's because it's not natural. I'm not saying it's bad, I'm just saying that leaving your family regularly for months at a time is not natural. I did not get married and have kids so that I could spend time *away* from them. I got married and had kids so I could spend time *with* them. That's the natural order. Leaving them for months at a time was not natural.

Needless to say, this is at least one of the reasons that divorce and marital strife are commonplace in the military. Unnatural things have unnatural consequences. I will say though that the military is keenly aware of the stress that deployments put on the family. This is not me being facetious; I really did experience that reality. Commanding Officers worried about the toll deployments took on their subordinates and did what they could to mediate that. The military, as a whole, did so as well. In fact, there is an entire protocol in the lead-up both to deployments and homecomings that all units follow to help assist families with these difficult realities. These protocols are engaged both pre- and post-deployment. And I think they probably do help a bit. They can't help everyone or every situation, but nothing is a panacea.

Why am I telling you this? To illustrate my initial point about operationalizing my constructs so that we are on the same sheet of music about these important terms. I remember clearly that I was leading a post-deployment exercise designed to ease military members back into the "normalcy" of home life after an extended combat deployment. The group in question was a platoon of EOD Marines. We were conducting what is referred to in the military as a "Return and Reunion" brief. The idea is to help the Marine or Sailor ease back into the normal routine of family life after being in a very abnormal situation for the past six months or a year. Of all of the programs the military has (and there are a lot of them), this is one of the most effective.

In this case, it was limited to the EOD Marines (Explosive Ordnance Disposal) because they had had a particularly arduous deployment in a very dangerous field. And what most people don't realize is that, while coming home from deployment is not as difficult as leaving for one, it is not easy. Six months is a long time. A year is even longer. The service member gets used to doing things a certain way, and the family gets used to doing things a certain way. Those ways are not always compatible once you get home. So this program is designed to help the Sailor or Marine transition and integrate back into a normal life.

In this particular case, we were discussing the importance for the service member to not simply just walk in and think things are going to be exactly as they were when they left. Their family has gotten used to the service member being gone. They have developed routines and ways of doing things that best helped them cope with the separation. One of the worst things a service member can do is then to walk in, assert their presence, and think things are going to go back to the way they were before. This guarantees that the family will bristle at this, get frustrated, and begin to wonder why it was they wanted the service member back in the first place. This approach is not good for the service member, not good for the family, and not good for the marriage. And a distressed marriage is not good for the military. So you can see the reasoning behind this approach.

In this case, however, there was a problem. One of the senior enlisted members of the group, a Gunnery Sergeant (or Gunny, as they are affectionately known), decided to share his philosophy on return and reunion. Gunny started telling everyone in the room about his "old lady" and how they didn't have any issues when he got back from deployments. He then enlightened us on how these returns were not a problem for his marriage. Simply put, Gunny told us that he comes home after a deployment, announces to his wife that he is back, and tells her that he doesn't care how she was doing things while he was gone and that things were going to go exactly as he mandated. And he told us that, since he laid down the law of the land to his "old lady," there weren't any issues.

Now, I have nothing but respect for the senior enlisted members of the military. It sounds cliché, but that does not detract from the truth that they are the backbone of the military. But if Gunny was trying his best to give out the worst advice he could ever give, then he couldn't have topped what he said that day. Now, I had to point out this stupidity without disrespecting the Gunny. I had a feeling I was right about something, so I began to ask some pretty innocuous questions, hoping to get the answer that I was looking for. Eventually, I did ask the right question because Gunny volunteered that he was on his third marriage. I had made my point.

But to be clearer still, once he left the room, I pointedly told everyone in that room that Gunny's definition of return and reunion was not the one that I was working with. See what I mean? Gunny and I were both talking about return and reunion. We used the same terms, shared the same service, deployed to the same place. But there were two entirely different definitions of return and reunion. I had to operationalize my construct to those around me, so that those who were listening to me would not confuse Gunny's definition of return and reunion with mine. That's why we took this short journey — to explain that it is not enough to simply see the words on the Marriage Pyramid and apply them to whatever myriad of definitions might be available, but to make these constructs clear so that we both know what I am talking about when I use these words. Again, you may not agree, but you will know where I am coming from. That's why we had the lengthy conversation about love. And that's why we are going to apply this idea to explaining one of the most important yet most misunderstood aspects of the marriage relationship: safety.

Jesus, marriage...and safety?

I bet I know what you're thinking. You're probably thinking that, by safety, I mean the rudimentary elements of safety, such as adequate food and shelter or, more likely, physical safety at the hands of your spouse. In other words, when I begin my explanation of this topic, most assume that I am going to discuss physical safety from the standpoint of telling folks that if you engage in mental or physical abuse towards your spouse, your marriage relationship will suffer irreparable harm. But come on, do we really need to spend an inordinate amount of time trying to prove this? Really?

When I was leading the CREDO Marriage Enrichment Retreats in my Navy days, I dedicated a huge section of the program to a module I entitled "Relationship Killers." I have included a chapter with this title where I will explore these things in more detail later. But I will touch on the constructs here a bit now to give context to the idea of safety as it relates to the Marriage Pyramid. I know 'Relationship Killers" is not the most positive or whimsical title, but it is a true title. I wanted for these folks to hear the truth about what could kill their relationship much more than I wanted them to smile at a cute title. Be that as it may, it was always one of the more interesting modules we covered. Mainly because everyone was convinced I was going to spend the bulk of my time talking about what I referred to as the "Big Three." The three things that logically fall into this category are physical abuse, substance abuse, and adultery. I call these the Big Three because they are the ones that are most visible and will certainly kill any relationship that includes them. However, while these are the most visible relationship killers, in my experience, they were not the predominant reasons that most of my couples were having issues. Oh, I dealt with them on a somewhat consistent basis, but they were by far in the minority among the reasons married couples ended up in my office.

And let's be honest, if I have to spend a large amount of time basically telling grown married folks that physical abuse, substance abuse, or adultery will destroy your relationship, then we have bigger problems to worry about. I think we all have our heads screwed on pretty good about this. If I had to do a segment called "Hitting Your Spouse Does Harm to Your Marriage," then shouldn't I follow it up with such important classes as "The Sun is Hot" and "Falling Off Mt. Everest will Probably Hurt You?" I had precious few hours with these couples to illustrate to them the potential dangers to their marriage, so I mentioned the obvious ones and hammered on the less obvious and more prevalent ones. Such is the case with safety. And while physical safety is an absolute necessity, I don't need to convince people of this. I need to alert them to the danger that lurks in the background. The quiet danger waiting to chip away and erode a relationship without the couple even knowing it is there. So the safety I am referring to is not just physical safety but emotional safety. And if you don't think this is that important, let me explain.

When you choose to love someone to the point where you will end up marrying him or her, that is the most powerful love one human being can bestow upon another. You give yourself to them, and they give themselves to you. This relationship, by the way (according to Genesis), supersedes the parent-child relationship. It's not better, just different. Note when God performs the very first marriage ceremony between Adam and Eve, the text exclaims, "Therefore man shall leave his father and mother and be joined to his wife, and they shall become one flesh" (Genesis 2:24). It is also of the utmost importance that we see the extraordinary significance God places on the marriage relationship in how it is used symbolically of Jesus' relationship with His church.

One of the most important passages of Scripture in the entire Bible is often obscured by one of the most misunderstood passages in all of the Bible. We won't revisit that controversial passage here because we already pointed out the fallacious portrayals of the verse that states, "Wives, submit to your own husbands as to the Lord" (Eph. 5:22, NKJV). Again, we put the foolishness surrounding this passage to rest earlier in chapter one. But what so often happens when foolishness invades the reading of God's Word is that we focus so much on the folly that we miss the grace. Such is the case with the fifth chapter of Ephesians.

So much ink is spilled and breath expelled in trying to calm people's misconceptions about the whole "submit" thing that we neglect the wonder found in that very same chapter. I would like to think that this is simply just a side effect of the foolishness but, knowing the Adversary the way we should, this seems an intentional act of misdirection to keep us from really seeing not only how God views marriage, but how much He treasures us. Let's take a quick look at what I mean.

After Paul writes that wives should submit to their own husbands "as to the Lord" (a part often left out), he then immediately begins to explain what that looks like and how it works. He does so by quickly shifting attention away from the wife and to the husband. In fact, in that entire collection of passages, only 3.5 verses even mention the wife. The other 8.5 verses focus on the husband. So, in reality, the passage that many people seem to think is directed at wives is, in fact, way more directed at husbands. We see this implied even more clearly when the wife is commanded by Paul to submit and respect her husband, and the husband is commanded to love his wife. It is interesting to note that the wife is not commanded to love her husband. I wonder why that might be? We'll get to that in a bit.

And once we see how Paul then directs attention away from the wife and towards the husband, he also includes an extraordinary treatise of Christ and how He plays a role in all of this. After Paul commands that a husband should love his wife, he then compares that love with the love Christ has for His church. Paul writes, "that He might sanctify and cleanse her with the washing of water by the word, that He might present her to Himself a glorious church, not having spot or wrinkle or any such thing, but that she should be holy and without blemish" (Ephesians 5:26-27, NKJV).

This is groundbreaking here and, more importantly, it is God allowing us to see how important the marriage relationship is by comparing that relationship to the relationship Jesus has with His church. I hope you're seeing the magnitude of this. And just in case any of us might miss this, Paul doubles down on it later in the same chapter. After Paul quotes Genesis 2:24 (where the two shall become one flesh), a passage clearly delineating the essence of the marriage relationship, he then continues by writing, "This is a great mystery, but I speak concerning Christ and the church" (Ephesians 5:31-32). Do you see what Paul is doing here, under the guidance of the Holy Spirit? He is using the human marriage relationship as the real-world symbol of Christ's relationship with His very own church.

This is astounding. Of all of the possible analogies He could have used to paint this precious picture of how we are to view Jesus' relationship with His church, He used marriage. This is not the only place He does so. We see this same analogy in John 3:29, Matthew 9:14-15, Mark 2:18-20, Luke 5:33-35, Revelation 22:17, 2 Corinthians 11:2, John 2:9, Revelation 19:7, Ephesians 5:25-27, and Revelation 21:2. I really hope you see the implications of this reality, because it does two very important things. This analogy show the intimacy of the love that Christ has for His church. And it shows how important marriage is to God. The relationship Jesus has with His church is exactly the relationship spouses should have with each other. At least, that is the model we strive towards. Sin will always cause us to fall short, but this model is not presented so that we will try harder or do better, but so that we see how important marriage is to God and, consequently, how important it should be to us.

That's the entire idea behind the Marriage Pyramid in the first place. The culture has presented marriage as a disposable commodity, easily joined into and just as easily dissolved. This mentality has spawned the ridiculous (and dangerous) construct known as "starter marriages." Borrowing the old term we used to use for houses, this idea suggests that it is perfectly alright to enter into a marriage at the beginning of your marrying era with the idea that you will, more than likely, not stay married to that person. In fact, you should probably plan to not stay in this starter marriage any more than you would plan to stay in a starter home. This mentality devalues marriage to the point that it has virtually no value in our community. That is the goal, by the way. Attacking humanity by attacking the marriage relationship is not a new reality.

In fact, it began thousands of years ago when the Adversary approached Eve. If you remember, it was only after Eve was created that the serpent went after that relationship. His intent was to encourage disobedience and drive a wedge between the very first married couple in history. It is then no surprise that we see that fall into sin include a curse that clearly states there will be permanent discord between husbands and wives (Genesis 3:16c). That is why it is of the utmost importance to understand how safety factors into the marriage relationship and that without it, even if we have the love, we will never be able to move beyond that rung of the Pyramid to the marriage God has for us.

You see here the importance of the husband/wife relationship, as described in the Bible. In no other human relationship are we called to become "one flesh" with another person, and that includes parents. This is extremely important to understand in the context of discussing this issue of safety. We'll expound on that later. No other relationship is used to describe the connection between Christ and the church except the marriage relationship. Suffice it to say that the close personal relationship between a husband and wife is paramount to any other human relationship.

That's why the subject of safety is paramount. It's not one we think about consciously very often, and that's not a good thing. This view of safety is elusive because it sneaks up on us in such a way that, when we finally recognize its importance, it is generally too late. That being said, here is how I describe this safety aspect of the pyramid.

Safe and sound?

Choosing to love my spouse, with the love I explained earlier, makes me extremely vulnerable. Does it not? Think about it. I have known my wife since I was six years old. We've been married nearly 30 years. She is the best friend I have or have ever had. And she knows absolutely everything about me. She knows the good, the not so good, the bad. She knows my weaknesses. That is part and parcel of what it means to be married. I don't find comfort in my weaknesses — none of us ever should. But what my wife does for me is to encourage me to be aware of them and rise above them. That is part of what makes her my wife. But it is also a precarious situation to be in. It is a bit unnerving to have so much invested in someone who knows my most significant weaknesses.

She knows my fears. This one is really scary. Call me old-school, but I still ascribe to the idea that I am my wife's knight in shining armor. I am the dragon slayer. I am the one that, when it's time to move forward into uncharted territories, should be blazing the trail and making it safe. But I'm afraid sometimes. My children don't see my fear. My friends don't see my fear. My congregants and readers don't see my fear. My extended family doesn't see my fear. My wife? She sees my fear. She sees it more than I care for sometimes. She knows what keeps me up at night and what drives me to the paralysis of inaction. I am her knight, but she knows when I'm afraid to put on the armor. She also knows that I put it on anyway. In large part because she does know my fears and knows what to do to allay them. But what if she didn't want to allay them? What if she wanted to stoke them? How safe would I feel?

She knows what hurts me and why. To continue my analogy, though I may wear the armor, she knows where the vulnerabilities are. One of the most precious aspects of being married is that spouses share just about everything. And one of the most poignant elements we share is our pain. We all carry some measure of pain in our lives. In my life, there is only one person on the planet who knows all of mine. My bride has heard and seen the pain I carry from many unfortunate incidents in life. As I said, we all have them. Having someone to love and help us nurse those injuries is a blessing beyond belief. The best part? Even though she knows my hurts, she loves me anyway. Even when they manifest themselves in unpleasant ways. But there is another side to this coin, right? What if, along with bearing my pain with me, she used that information to harm me? I don't mean all the time. But what if, during the middle of a heated argument where she might find herself in a one-down position, she decided to use that information to inflict pain. How safe do you think I would feel then?

In other words, what I am saying is, if she wanted to, she could hurt me more than anyone else in the world. She could, right? I mean, as I said, she knows every fear and weakness I have. It stands to reason then that, if she knows these fears and weaknesses, then she could exploit them to hurt me. She could, as I stated just a moment ago, hurt me more than anyone else in the world, even more than our kids could. And that means I am extremely vulnerable to her. She could hurt me, but I am counting on the fact that she won't. That is part of the deal with love. You are betting that this person who *could* hurt you the most *won't*. But the very fact that she holds this position in my life leads to one inescapable and paradoxical conclusion. And that is that my wife, the love of my life, is potentially the most dangerous person in the world to me. It stands to reason, right? If there is a person that could hurt you more than anyone else in the world, then by default that person becomes, potentially, the most dangerous person to you in the world. And if they are the most dangerous person to you, then that is because they can hurt you more than anyone else can. Ergo, that person is, potentially, the most dangerous person in the world to you. And you're married to that person. Let that sink in a minute.

If I make the claim that no one in the world could hurt me more than my wife, if she chose to do so, that makes her not only dangerous, but the most dangerous person in the world to me, potentially. I simply trust the fact that she will not do that. Now, I'm not merely talking about arguing. All couples argue, and mostly over stupid things. And merely arguing with my wife is not enough to trigger this "most dangerous person" toggle in our relationship... unless. And it is this "unless" where the insidious danger to the emotional safety of the couple lives, breathes, and attacks. Let me explain further what I mean by this.

If there has been one consistency in the troubles of the relationships I have dealt with over the years, it is the use of catastrophic statements during arguments. I delve into this phenomenon in more detail later in the book. And in case you are not sure what I mean by catastrophic, let me give an example. If you are in an argument with your spouse, and you use the phrases "you always" or "you never," it doesn't matter what comes after that — it is most probably a lie. Because nobody "always" does something (unless it's breathing) and people do not "never" do things either (unless it's not going to Mars). Let me give you some advice about what is going on in the head of your spouse when you use the term "you always" in an argument by presenting a scenario that has been all too real in our household. We'll use a fairly innocuous example that we can all sort of chuckle at because most of us have been there. Here we go:

My bride: **"You *always* leave your clothes on the floor."**

Me: (knowing this is mostly true, but also knowing it is not completely true, immediately searches my mind for a time six

67

weeks ago when I actually picked up my   clothes)   **"I do not always leave my clothes on the floor... six weeks ago I picked them up."**

My bride: **"Well I didn't mean literally *always*."**

Me: **"Well, that's what you said."**

My bride: **"That's not what I meant. You know what I mean."**

Me: **"Yeah, you're right, I've been able to read your mind for years. Why don't you say what you mean?"**

My bride: **"Well, you don't say what you mean either. What about the time you said..."**

Me: **"Well you've said worse that that. Remember 8 years ago when you..."**

See where we're headed here? And three hours later, once the argument is over, neither of us could possibly tell you what started it in the first place. My bride is mostly correct. I do leave my clothes on the floor a lot (though I have gotten better). But I am not going to focus on the real problem, am I? Instead, I am going to focus on the fact that she communicated that I *always* leave my clothes on the floor. Now, I really do know what she means, but I am not going to go there. I am going to focus on the verbiage to redirect the argument away from me, to her. That's called being human. Our sin encourages us to do these things because our pride does not want to let us see whatever shortcomings we may have. Now, this is a pretty harmless example of a catastrophic statement.

If I do this to my wife or she does it to me, neither of us is going to think the other is threatening the safety of the relationship. But there are others. And they can be sneaky… and dangerous.

The most prevalent example I have seen of this and the damage it has done is when one spouse or the other (or sometimes both) actually threatens the safety of the relationship while making these catastrophic statements. If I love my wife with the love I have described up to this point, and if I am that vulnerable to her as I have described, and if she is potentially the most dangerous person to me, then the most devastating thing she can do to me is to end our relationship. If she walked away from this, it is safe to say that I would never again be the same. All of those vulnerabilities will have been attacked, and I will be left irreparably harmed. Ending and destroying the relationship is the worst thing my bride could do to me. I will expand that to say that one spouse ending the relationship is the single most emotionally dangerous thing that one spouse can do to another (remember, I am not comparing this to physical abuse; we went over the fact that physical abuse is horrible and will definitely destroy the relationship). In a relatively healthy marriage with none of the Big Three, ending the relationship and/or threatening the safety of the relationship is the most dangerous thing that can happen.

Think about it this way: if my wife, in the heat of an argument, hints at, suggests, or outright threatens divorce in any way, shape, or form, something weird happens. Follow this, because this is important. And remember, we are working on the premise that my wife is *potentially* the most dangerous person in the world to me. If my wife threatens the safety of the relationship, she goes from *hypothetically* being the most dangerous person in the world to me to actually *becoming* the most dangerous person. Remember, no one can hurt me more than her. And the worse thing she can do to me is threaten the marriage. So the most (hypothetically) dangerous person in the world has now threatened me with the most hurtful thing they can hurt me with. Ergo, she has become the most dangerous person in the world to me. The transformation is complete, and I now have been threatened by the most dangerous person with the worst thing. I am no longer emotionally, relationally, or matrimonially safe.

And what happens when our safety is threatened? We will fight to feel safe again. I can't tell you how important this construct is. It is a foundational belief element from a biological standpoint, but we don't correlate that with emotional safety. Not doing so is a huge mistake. Even Dr. Maslow, in his Hierarchy of Needs, places basic safety-related needs at the foundation of his pyramid. He lists things like having food, water, and safe housing as the elemental items we desperately need if we are to have any semblance of a life at all. The one thing those elements have in common is the idea that we need those things to live. We need them to feel safe from starving to death, dehydrating to death, and dying from exposure to the realities of a harsh world. According to a great number of psychologists, sociologists, and biologists, the drive to stay alive and safe is the strongest human drive we have. This drive bleeds over to other things that could possibly harm or kill us in a very significant way. When our safety is threatened, we will strive diligently, even desperately, to feel safe.

We don't have to think about it. We don't have to reason it out. If you are on a boat and you can't swim and you fall out of the boat within arm's reach of a flotation device, you will immediately clamor and struggle to that device. You won't say, "Well, I can't swim. And the life preserver is just past my grasp. I guess I'm done for." No. Despite the fact that you cannot swim, your life is in danger and you will scramble for safety immediately, without even thinking about. When we feel unsafe, our natural reaction is to feel safe again. It is human nature. It is what we do.

It's the same in marriage when your emotional safety is threatened. If my wife threatens to end our marriage, I am feeling the most emotionally unsafe that I can feel. I am in more emotional danger than I can be. I have fallen into the water, and I cannot swim. That being the case, I will scramble for safety. And since my wife has become dangerous to me, I have to ask a very important question. Under these circumstances, am I going to scramble towards her for this safety (which is what I would do if I was feeling unsafe for some other reason)? Think about this question before you answer it. If I felt unsafe for any reason other than one involving my wife, she would be the first person I would run to. She would, normally, be my life preserver. However, now she is the source of the danger. She is threatening me with the worst thing (emotionally) that can happen to me. She has moved from *potentially* being the most dangerous person in the world to me to actually *becoming* that threat. Under those circumstances, in my scramble to feel safe, will I naturally gravitate towards her?

No, of course not. She is the source of my danger. She is the threat. I don't need her to help me with the danger because she *is* the danger. Why would I go to her? In fact, it is the exact opposite. Like any danger I will face (physical or otherwise), I will want to remove myself from the danger, not run headlong into it. No rational person does this. No, I will distance myself from that danger (her) as fast as I can. Remember, the goal is to feel safe again from this tremendous threat. That is what we do as human beings. Of course, there are jobs that lead people to run into danger, such as the military, law enforcement, and firefighting. I get that. But even they will tell you that the thing that separates them from others is their willingness to do what is not natural: move towards danger and unsafety. We're talking about the natural course of events that transpire under normal conditions with rational people. And rational people scramble for safety in unsafe

71

conditions. What's more? We don't have to think about it, we just do it. We don't have to think about it anymore than we have to think about reaching for a life preserver in water when we can't swim. Simply put, I will try to take the emotional high ground so that she cannot hurt me anymore. And if I have to do so at her expense, I will. Because the driving desire to be safe trumps absolutely everything else. She will, for all intents and purposes, become my enemy, and I will do and say what I have to in order to distance myself from her. See what I'm saying?

I am telling you this because, of all of the catastrophic statements you can make to your spouse, suggesting that this relationship is on tenuous footing and could end will not get your spouse to listen to you or take you seriously. I have seen this time and again. And in my experiences, I have seen this tenfold more that the Big Three combined. I have had hundreds of couples in my office, and the vast majority of them had no reason at all to be considering divorce. Most of the time, one thing kept coming up again and again. One spouse or the other, in the middle of continued arguments, will either explicitly or implicitly threaten divorce. The explicit threats are obvious: "maybe we should just get divorced," "I'm taking the kids and leaving." The implicit ones are more subtle and maybe more dangerous: "I can't take this much longer," "I don't know how much longer I can go on." The receiver of this message really has only one conclusion to draw: my spouse is going to leave me. And when she/he reaches that conclusion, they will scramble for safety and do so at the expense of their spouse.

You want to know the most depressing part of this? The vast majority of time, the spouse threatening divorce doesn't really mean it. I know this because they have told me this. They will tell me, "It's the only way he will listen to me" or "It's the only way she will take me seriously." Believe me when I tell you that I more than feel the pain of spouses who have felt this way and uttered these words. Sometimes, it is not easy being married. Expectations are not met and disillusionment sets in. I get it. But the gains you believe you are making by either overtly or implicitly threatening divorce during the middle of difficult times are an illusion.

Let's say you're right. Let's say you're in a marriage relationship with someone who, for the most part, does not really listen to or acknowledge your concerns about the marriage. At least, not in the way you want them too. This can take place in a variety of ways. And let's also say that, at times, your more-than-justifiable frustration boils over, and you give in to the temptation to suggest that the marriage could be on the brink of dissolution, even if you don't really mean it. Once more, let's also say that, when you do this, the troublesome spouse immediately snaps-to and begins to listen in a way that previously did not happen. You conclude that all you have to do is utter this threat (again, either implicitly or explicitly), and he/she will heed you and begin listening. Have you ever wondered why this takes place? It takes place because the safety of the relationship is threatened, and the person will do whatever they think is feasible to regain that safety. It will start by responding to the threatening spouse in a way that might be best to preserve the relationship. It will not stay that way. Because the question we need to be asking (along with, "Why do the threats seem to be the only way to show my spouse that I'm serious?") is, "How long is this going to work?"

Let me give you a real-life example of how this phenomenon often plays out. Over the years and a plethora of clients, it has been rare that I remember *specific* counseling cases. The specific details and faces associated with these sessions have sort of just melted into the background, like a Jackson Pollock painting. I remember all of the underlying issues and constructs because they generally fell into a few identifiable and quantifiable categories. But with hundreds upon hundreds of sessions, the specifics of any one case, for the most part, are pretty much lost to the nether regions of my mind. Except for a few. This is one of those few.

This couple came into my office, as so many couples did, while I was assigned to a USMC unit. It doesn't matter which one. In sizing them up, I assumed that this would be a typical session (or sessions, as it would turn out) with typical issues. I was right. It was every bit of a "typical" (depending on how you define that) counseling session with a relatively young Marine Corps married couple. To this day, I cannot tell you why this one sticks out in my mind. There are so many details I still remember, and I am convinced that if I saw either of them walking down the street, I would be able to point them out. First of all, they were not kids. And yes, I know the definition of that term expands the older I get, but what I mean is that they were not late teens/early twenties with barely a year of married life under their belt. I deal with a lot of those folks, but this wasn't the case here. They were both in their early thirties with two young kids and had been married about 6-9 years, if memory serves.

Two things immediately jumped out at me. First is how likable the husband turned out to be. You know the type. Gregarious, outgoing, witty, and with a dynamic personality. He was an instantly likable person. He was very popular with his command and a hard worker. He always had a great story, joke, or anecdote tucked away in his brain. He was sort of a big kid at heart. He had an infectious smile and always had a quip at the ready. You could tell that, even though he was a good worker, he didn't take anything really all that seriously. That was the first thing I noticed about him.

The second thing I noticed about him was that I immediately came to the conclusion that he would be a nightmare to be married to. All of the traits I mentioned above are great to be around, unless you're married to that person. He was great with the kids, but that was because he was a big kid. So, in essence, his wife had three children instead of two. And for the record, I came to this conclusion, not because the wife told me so, but because it was painfully obvious after spending about 10 minutes with this guy. In other words, I felt her pain. In fact, in all of the years I have dealt with married couples, this was one of the very few times where I felt that the lion's share of the "blame" for the marital woes fell on one person, as opposed to it being (mostly) evenly split. That's not to say that the wife was without culpability, but I was way more sympathetic to her than to him. I really did feel for her because he was such a likable guy, it couldn't help but make her out to be the "bad guy." That's certainly the way she felt.

And this emerged even more clearly the more we engaged. She was a very nice person who wanted to be married to her husband but was unhappy about significant parts of the marriage. And she had every right to feel that way. Her husband also acknowledged she had the right to feel that way. The wife then proceeded to elaborate on the cycle of dysfunction that enveloped their lives. Things would be ok for a while, until some of the little things would evolve into not-so-little things which would evolve into bigger things. The wife would snap, an argument would ensue, there would be pledges to change, and things would go back to being ok for a while again. And so it would go. The cycle is familiar, and so were the issues. There were none of the Big Three or any other overtly toxic actions. The complaints centered around the husband not helping with the house, not taking her seriously, not helping with the kids, and not being a "grown-up" (however that was defined). This had been going on for years, and both parties recognized the issues. But the consistency of the unresolved issues would inevitably lead to the wife engaging in a less-than-helpful (but fully understandable) course of action.

Whenever the situation got to a boiling point, the wife still had to deal with the fact that, not only was she very frustrated, but this frustration was multiplied tenfold by her husband's sort of laissez-faire approach to marriage in general and marital problems in particular. In other words, he had gotten so used to the cycle and the complaints that he began (if he actually ever did in the first place) to not take them overly seriously. He simply had factored in the cycle of dysfunction as a part of their "normal" marital relationship. He assumed this way of existing was just sort of the norm and that, like always, the storm would eventually pass. Yeah, his wife would get angry or frustrated. But she would also "get over it," and they could get back to where things were before. However, he was gravely mistaken. While his wife was certainly willing to tolerate this existence for a while (a fairly long while, in fact), she was reaching the end of the proverbial rope. Because her husband had gotten so used to the complaints, he began to pay only lip-service to fixing them. He was not, in the mind of his wife, taking them seriously. She then had to come up with a way to assist him, so that he would take them seriously. She began threatening divorce.

Understand, I do not believe this was a manipulative maneuver as much as it was a maneuver of desperation. And she did not begin by explicitly vocalizing the threat. At first, the threat was more of a subtle insinuation. She would use certain words and phrases that would casually suggest the possibility that a lack of change could lead to a dissolved marriage. She would say things like, "I can't take much more of this," "I don't know how much longer I can go on like this," "we can't keep going like this." Again, all certainly understandable reactions for someone feeling as desperate as she was feeling. The idea here is not to suggest that the wife is to be singled out for blame. Her reactions are completely understandable and should evoke our sympathy. And these implicit threats did seem to have an effect on her husband for a while. Until even they became part of the cycle. This led the wife to even higher levels of frustration and, therefore, more desperate verbiage. The husband had begun to ignore the implicit threats, which then inevitably led to explicit threats in order to try and save the marriage. Because that is all the wife wanted to do. She simply wanted her marriage to be able to survive; that's it. And while her goal was admirable, she embarked upon a methodology that would invoke one of the most important and reliable laws in the universe: the law of unintended consequences.

I solemnly believe that, in the pantheon of decisions we will make in our lifetime, the single most important caveat we ignore while administering these decisions is the law of unintended consequences. In other words, we embark on a decision that we feel is the correct one (and in fact, it may be) without understanding that there will be second- and third-order effects because of the decision. I decided to join the Navy. It was the right decision because it was a decision ordained by God. It was His will. However, there were a multitude of effects on my life, my family, my finances, my theology, my... everything. Many of the consequences I anticipated, some of them I did not. Many of the consequences were a natural flow from the realities of being in the military, but some of them were the also-natural unintended consequences of that life choice. We cannot escape unintended consequences — that's why they're designated as unintended. But we do have to be aware of them as best we can. That's where this wife made her mistake.

She discovered that, while her implicit threats of divorce were quickly losing their impact, her explicit threats were becoming more effective. It is, of course, completely understandable that a person would alter a course of action when that one became ineffective. That is exactly what this wife decided

77

to do. Once the hints of divorce became mundane and were having less of an impact, she resorted to explicit and overt threats of divorce in order to convince her husband to "take her seriously." She discovered quickly that this new course of action was very effective. Her husband did, very much, begin to take her seriously. He paid more attention to what was being said and seemed more engaged with the issues that were causing marital strife. It's not that things were really getting all that better, but he did seem to "care" more when active threats of divorce became the de facto "Popeye" moment. In fact, it was these threats that drove the couple to my office and into counseling in the first place. But as "successful" as she may have seemed to be, she very much did not anticipate the possibility of unintended consequences.

Like the vast (and I mean *vast*) majority of married couples around the world today, this wife had never even contemplated this entire idea we've been discussing. It never occurred to her to think of herself as potentially the most dangerous person in the world to her husband. In fact, I believe that if I had tried to convince her of that, she would have quickly concluded that I was certifiably insane. I do know this, however: she did not want to get a divorce from her husband. I know this because she told me so. I counseled them over a number of sessions, both as a couple and individually. And every time I spoke individually with the wife, she told me over and over again that she did not *really* want a divorce but that her husband would only take her seriously if she threatened it. She was right, but that tactic also led to the very consequence she was trying to avoid.

This is one of the many times I saw this idea of emotional safety take a horrendous toll on a marriage. I kept telling the wife that she either needed to divorce her husband, or stop threatening it. Though she was having a difficult time believing it, I tried my best to tell her that this tactic would eventually cause way more harm than she originally intended. The reason that this inevitable harm was destined to arise is because, in his attempt to feel emotionally safe, the husband would eventually do so at the expense of his wife. Remember what we've already said. Once a person has been threatened by the person who is potentially the most dangerous person in the world, the natural reaction is to scramble for safety. Continuing the analogy I was using earlier, the husband had been tossed overboard and was desperately striving for safety. And just like we would never scramble *towards* the source of the danger, but will, in fact, scramble *away* from that source, that is exactly what began to happen with the husband.

The initial times I would talk to the husband individually would include genuine sorrow (often to the point of tears) and genuine fear. One day, however, all of that changed. His demeanor completely altered, and I detected a sort of fatalistic malaise that had washed over him. He had no more tears, and he had no more angst. He stated to me very quietly and calmly (though very morosely) that he had given up. He said, "She keeps telling me she is leaving and taking the kids. I just have to accept the fact that she's gone, and there's nothing I can do." He had finally succumbed to the reality that his wife was now a danger to him. In fact, emotionally, she was the most dangerous person in the world to him because she was capable of inflicting, emotionally, the most dangerous actions upon him. And those actions included leaving him and taking the kids. He had firmly settled into survival mode. His danger was at the highest level he could imagine. As a result, he instinctively began to protect himself, as best he could, from the most dangerous person in the world to him — his wife. And the worst part was that his wife did not really want the divorce. She simply, and understandably, just wanted him to listen and change. But he could not see past the threats. He could not reason past the fear. The desire, if there was any, for repairing this wounded relationship gave way to one simple, unavoidable, and inescapable reality: safety. He simply wanted to feel safe, especially with the one person designed to provide that level of safety: his wife.

And now that she had become the most dangerous person, emotionally, in the world to him, she became a person he needed to be protected from. He needed to feel safe, and the only way he could do that was to distance himself from her, as much as he possibly could. He could not allow her to inflict any more damage to him. So he insulated himself from her in any way that he could. He grasped onto the life preserver — only the lifesaving entity wasn't her. It was, in fact, in spite of her. And the "positives" she thought she was getting from the overt threats of divorce disappeared in a haze of indifference and antipathy. You see, those are the weapons of defense against emotional danger. You cannot be hurt if you do not care. And the husband engaged these weapons in a way that only the terminally hurt can do. He nearly completely withdrew from his wife and their situation, because to engage simply meant being put more at risk. The threats led to more threats, which led to a lack of safety, which led to fear, which led to active defense, which led to... divorce. Not long after our sessions ended, I was told that this couple (who did NOT want to divorce) ended up terminating their marriage. The exact opposite of what both persons wanted ended up coming to fruition. And this couple then simply became a data point in a very large body of statistics.

Some advice.

I know what you're thinking (especially if you are a wife): what was she supposed to do, under the circumstances? This seems like a no-win situation. Truth is, I'm not sure what she was supposed to do. I wish it were that simple. I really do. I wish I could tell you, now that we've discussed this issue, that I have a 5-step process for you to follow in order to avoid this happening to you and your spouse. If I told you that, I'd be lying to you. If anyone else tries to tell you they have a multi-step process to guarantee success in marriage, they're lying to you. While most marital problems are fairly universal and similarly foundational, the nuances and complexities involved in how these problems manifest themselves are vast. In other words, people pretty much do the same stupid things. It's one of the things that unites us as a species. However, how those stupid things manifest themselves and how they affect people are myriad. The complexities of our nuances argue against a one-size-fits-all approach to just about anything, but that especially includes marital relationships. However, that doesn't mean that I do not have some equally foundational advice based on the issues I have addressed as a counselor and that I have tried to incorporate into my own marriage. These are broad and elemental, but I believe that also equates them to being adaptable in a variety of circumstances. So let's take a look at a few.

First, I will suggest that we try not to engage in what I call panic negotiations. If you'll remember, earlier, I proposed that distressed marriages generally follow a very predictable cycle. This idea is not unique to me. Many experts in the field have discussed what some call a "cycle of dysfunction." The cycle applies generally to just about every marriage, in a more natural and not-as-destructive way. However, for more stressed marriages, the cycle can be easily observed as it moves the couple from one stage to another. These couples go from things being pretty good, to them being just ok, to them being not good, to them being bad, to a large blow-up argument, to words of apology and contrition, back to being pretty good. Then it all starts again, in the vein of wash, rinse, repeat. This pattern, as I stated, becomes increasingly predictable, so that even those in the very center of it begin to recognize what stage they are in. Also, it is an exhausting cycle. And once the couple reaches the argument stage, they have actually lived through two less-than-optimal stages of things being not good and then actually being bad. Therefore, the good parts of the relationship are so far off of the map, it is as if they never existed.

The not good and bad stages are very clearly in the side view mirror. And you know what it says in the side view mirror: objects in the mirror are closer than they appear. So by the time they cycle into the blow-up argument stage, only the more recent memories related to the bad stages are fresh in the mind and in the heart. This leads to selective memory and an unhealthy dependence on feelings. Feelings are very, very powerful entities. They are especially powerful when they convince us of things that never really happened. It is this confluence of misguided feelings and fading memories that intensifies an already bad situation and guarantees it will go to worse. What do I mean by fading memories and misguided feelings? Simply put, your memory will convince you of things that are not true, and your misguided feelings will inspire you to say things that are not completely true.

Since what will be mostly on your mind is the last few weeks (months?) of the last two bad stages, you will then begin to characterize your entire relationship in those stages. In other words, you will focus your ire related to your spouse on the bad stuff to the detriment of the good. It makes sense. You're angry, and the good stages are a long time back (relatively speaking). Therefore, you begin to suggest, very clearly, that everything is wrong with your relationship and that your spouse is the one nearly solely responsible for that. But, we often forget the good stages and that there have been many great moments while being married to this person. That all fades with attention dominated by fading memories and misguided feelings. And these comments have consequences. If everything is absolutely terrible during this stage, what happens to all the nice things you might say during the good stage? They come not to mean as much.

So that is what I mean about panic negotiations. In my view, we pick the absolute worst times to talk about marital shortcomings because we choose to "discuss" them in the midst of the worst part of the cycle — when things seem a lot worse and we are the angriest. The issues that cause the blow-up arguments are still issues even during the good and ok times. But we are calmer in those times. We are less frustrated and less angry during those times. We feel better about our spouse during those times. We acknowledge that, even with the problems, there are some good things as well. With that being the case, does it not make more sense to engage in these conversations in the good times, as opposed to the bad? Think of it this way. If I asked you to choose (in general) a time to talk to someone about something important, which would you choose? Would you choose a time where you are at your angriest, when you are thinking the least clearly, when your perspective is skewed, and when you are at your unhappiest? Or would you choose a time where you are generally happy, when you are most at peace, when you are thinking clearly, and when you are optimistic about the subject. Of course, we would all choose the second circumstance. If that is the case, then why do we wait until the first criteria have firmly entrenched themselves in our lives before we try to "discuss" issues that are detrimental to our relationship?

That's why I call it panic negotiations. When we are in that state, we are panicky. Because of the above-mentioned realities, we are convinced that this thing we are discussing is the most horrendous thing there is, that it happens all the time, that it means my spouse doesn't care, and that it has to be corrected right now or nothing will ever be good and holy in the world again. Then something weird happens. Someone breaks down and apologizes, which leads to the other person apologizing. There may be some tears and some extra affection, which will inevitably lead back to the first stage where everything is good again. It also means that all of that emotional extremist language ends up not being taken seriously, because if nothing is ever going to be good again, then why is it good now?

The words concerning very real and very harmful issues that plague this marriage come to not mean anything. They just end up being things that are said when the spouse is mad and that eventually they will forget when things go back to being good again. Which means these issues are never resolved. The cycle gets more intense. The "good" stages grow shorter and shorter, while the "bad" ones begin to dominate. I think we know what ends up happening after that.

If I may suggest, maybe we simply need to talk about difficult things when we are at our best. Our words will almost certainly be softer, and our receptors will not be dialed up to extreme defense. Using the example of the couple above, how might the husband have reacted if the wife had, during the good times, encouraged her husband to be the hero she wants him to be? Short answer? I don't know. It may not have made any difference at all. But here is what I do know: her way did not and does not work. If your spouse is emotionally unsafe because of you, you will not move any higher in the Pyramid than the first stage. That will be the best you can hope for. And with all due respect to the Beatles, love is not *all* you need. We need to think about this issue of safety and how it relates to us having the marriage that we have. Eliminating panic negotiations (as best you can) can go a long way to alleviating safety issues in a marriage.

Secondly, let's address a fatal mistake the husband made in our example. As I have said before, I was 100% on the side of the wife in this case. This is the only time that I can remember being able to say that. The biggest mistake the husband made was that he never embraced the design of marriage. Remember, God designed marriage. As I stated at the beginning of this book, it was the first institution God ever created. It even predates the church. Not only did He create marriage, but He gave us the characteristics of the design He had for what a Godly husband should be and what a Godly wife should be. Paul expounds on this in more detail in the fifth chapter of Ephesians as we saw earlier. Though the pericope on marriage starts with a role that the wife should adhere to, the vast majority of that passage focuses on the design God created for a husband. It is intimidating, to say the least. I am to love and treat my wife as Jesus loved and treated His "bride," the church. There's just one problem — He's Jesus, and I'm not.

I will fall short of that lofty goal, though I wish that I didn't. And that's the key. My bride knows that I will not measure up to the Godly characteristics of a husband, as designed by God. However, she knows that I want to measure up. I have a desire to measure up. I long to measure up. She sees that (at least, I hope she does). And that alone will get her through the times I fall short of that design. The husband in the example I shared above? I doubt he ever had the desire to be the husband God designed him to be. I don't think he was capable, because I am convinced neither he nor his wife were Believers. And you can't fulfill the design for a husband outside of the will of the Designer. The husband wanted to be married, but he didn't want to do what a husband needed to do. He lacked the desire, the want-to, and I think that's what frustrated his wife more than anything. It's also important to note that this lack of desire, in and of itself, could also be viewed by the wife as a threat to her emotional safety, as well. If his surmised lack of desire threatens the relationship, then that means he is a threat to the relationship, and you see how all of this stuff is connected to each other. That's why this idea of emotional safety is so vital to the marriage relationship.

One of the more beautiful pictures of this desire is found in the Book of Ruth. Ruth was a stranger in a strange land, bound to her former mother-in-law, Hannah (Ruth's husband had died), with an almost supernatural devotion. Leaving her own home and her own family to travel to a land of strangers and certain destitution, Ruth found herself nearly homeless and starving. Until she met Boaz. Boaz was much older than Ruth, had nothing in common with Ruth, and had little to gain by helping Ruth. But Boaz not only helped her — he loved her, married her, and took care of her. The wife in my story above just wanted her own Boaz. Why? Because Boaz kept her safe and, like all spouses, she just wanted to feel safe. She wanted to be able to put her faith in her husband as Ruth had placed hers in Boaz. But here's the thing: Boaz *wanted* to be a good, Godly husband. It was his *desire*. Read the book. His desire to be the husband God designed practically drips from the pages. In fact, his redemption of Ruth in marriage is often seen as a precursor of Christ's redemption of us.

We can only be the spouse God designed us to be if we follow the mandates of the Designer. We cannot escape this. We will never be the spouse God wants us to be apart from a relationship with Him. You may ask, "Are you saying that there has never been a good spouse who was *not* a Christian?" I will answer that by saying, "It depends on your definition of 'good' spouse." If you are asking if I think there has ever been a "good" (however that is defined) marriage between, say, atheists, then I would say there have been those marriages that have been as good as they were capable of being. From the world's perspective, I'm sure there have been a multitude of "successful" or even "happy" marriages throughout history among those of little or no faith. But they will not have been the marriage that God designed. They simply can't be for obvious, logical reasons. Any design not designed by the Designer is not His design. Those are not my rules, they are God's rules. Please direct all complaints to Him. It is simply my job to tell you the truth. What you do with that truth is obviously between you and God. That's why I chose these two courses of action to assist couples in their desire to *not* become a danger to their spouse. The first one, panic negotiations, is a practical offering related to anyone, whether they are a Christian or not. The second is more foundational, from a theological perspective, in that it presupposes a relationship with God in order to accomplish it. Both are good. Both are helpful and both are necessary if we are to *keep* our spouses safe from the most dangerous person in the world, not *become* the most dangerous person in the world.

Final thoughts.

You've probably noticed that we have spent a good amount of time on these first two stages of the Marriage Pyramid. That is the way it was designed. If you'll notice, the lower down on the Pyramid, the wider the level. That, too, is by design. These first two stages, love and safety, require significant depth and treatment, if we are to understand how this entire thing works. These first two levels are foundational. So foundational, in fact, that I have often toyed with switching them with each other in the Pyramid. If we don't understand love, we will never have the marriage God wants us to have. If we do not understand the role that emotional safety plays in the successful marriage, we will never have a successful marriage. These first two levels have to be understood in order to even begin to grasp what it looks like to get to the top of the Pyramid.

These first two levels are also easier to define and explain in a more objective manner. Many of the things we have discussed, related to these two, are very quantifiable at an extremely easy level. The next two, not as much. It will be a bit more difficult to quantify these things verifiably. It will be a bit more difficult to "see" what this looks like. This, of course, has nothing to do with you. The burden to attempt to explain this entire paradigm in any sort of coherent way falls squarely on me. I tell you this just to let you know that these next two chapters should not be quite as quantifiable as the two previous ones. But pay close attention. Here is where we begin to see what marriage looks like through the eyes of the Designer. What it means to have an optimal marriage within the scope of God's design. It is very cool. It is the marriage I want to have. It describes the husband I want my wife to have. That being said, let's take a look.

Chapter Four
Growth

It won't look the same to everyone.

As I stated above, the first two levels of the Marriage Pyramid are a bit easier to describe because they more lend themselves to objective, observable scrutiny. That is just sort of the nature of the beast. And I hope you're beginning to see the logical progression that makes the Pyramid so (hopefully) effective. In fact, it is probably best viewed by beginning from the top of the structure and working your way down, in order to better see how this whole thing works. For example, you can't become one (the top level of the Pyramid) with a spouse with whom you do not grow. You cannot grow with a spouse you do not feel safe with. You cannot feel safe with someone you do not love. The entire idea behind this paradigm is that one builds on the other and that all of them must be in place for us to have the optimal marriage. And that we will never be able to move to the next level of the Pyramid until the basic requirements of the previous one are met. It can even be the case that we actually move up and down on the Pyramid throughout our marriage, depending on the circumstances.

For example, we can, theoretically, have a couple who spends the vast majority of the time at the top level of the Pyramid. They could, in fact, have the optimal marriage for them. That doesn't mean they do not have issues — it simply means that these issues are dealt with so effectively that they are able to claim the top level of the Pyramid as their predominant habitat. But let's say that, in the middle of this optimal marriage, one of the spouses engages in an adulterous relationship, and it comes to light. In the blink of an eye, they will plunge from the top level of the Pyramid to the bottom level (or worse, completely off the grid). They may still love their spouse, but they don't feel safe, which means they cannot bond by growing, which means they cannot experience what it means to "become one." Likewise, it will take a very long time just to feel safe again in order to re-climb the Pyramid to the point they were at before, if it ever happens. Such is the fluid nature of this model.

It just so happens that, since this is the case, the two lower but necessarily foundational levels of the structure are simply (in my view) easier to identify and easier to elaborate on. But we are past those now. Now we begin to venture into the areas that everyone wants to be in, but few understand exactly how to get there. Part of the problem I have seen multiple times, is that there seems to be a disconnect between their *view* of marriage and the *reality* of marriage. I have said for years that one reason there is so much dissatisfaction in marriages is that people seem to want a finished product at the beginning of the process. I usually put it like this: couples want a 20-year marriage in year 5. It simply does not work that way. It generally takes, give or take a year, 20 years to have a 20-year marriage. I am, to this day, bombarded with memories of couples I have worked with who were on the edge of divorce for no discernible reason other than the old "this isn't what I thought it would be" mantra. So many times I would implore them to hang on, keep working, be patient, only to have one or both of them walk away because of this extraordinarily unrealistic expectation.

So as we move on to the last two levels of the Pyramid, I will endeavor, as best I can, to make these elements as clear as possible, while also touting the flexibility with which they may be applied. These last two levels are intentionally malleable. What works as bonding and growing for one couple may not work for another. As such, this element naturally rejects any attempt to provide a multi-step process that will guarantee that the two of you are "bonding." Instead, I will try to provide guiding principles to illustrate the overarching aim of bonding, rather than providing you with a laundry list of effective actions to ensure that growing is actually taking place. And there is no better way to do that (in my view) than to start this discussion off with a story that reveals, not the "way to do it," but what it looks like when you've discovered this all-important aspect to reaching your optimal marriage.

In order to do this, we need to go back a few years. I would say about 5-7 years. My family and I were living in southeastern North Carolina, and I was stationed at Camp Lejeune, located in Jacksonville, North Carolina. In fact, I would spend my last nearly 7 years in the military at that duty station and in the home my wife and I shared with our four children. In order to grasp the totality of this story and how it relates to the idea of growing and bonding together, I first have to communicate to you part of our philosophy of child rearing. When the military is such a vital part of your life, you are forced to make certain decisions about things related to that reality. Since we moved around quite a bit during that time, we had to decide what we were going to do about childcare, if/when we decided to take time away as a couple. This idea of date nights and taking time away as a couple is extremely important in marriage. You can become so involved in the "doing" parts of having a family that you can often lose sight of the "being" part. Make any sense? Along with the always-hectic parts of parenting, it is essential that we remember that we also have to be a spouse to our wife/husband. If we forget that, there are prices to pay.

All that to say that once we had children and we knew that, as part of the military life, we would be (for the most part) hours away from family and very close lifelong friends, we had to decide how to balance time away as a couple with trustworthy and safe childcare for the kids. We came up with a very simple solution. We simply decided that ensuring the safety of our kids was more important than time away. This was a mutual decision that we came to, for the most part, instinctively. In other words, it's not like we had this big husband-wife meeting to gather the data, assess the pros and cons, and then adapt a suitable course of action. No, instead we were immediately like-minded about this and made our decisions based on this choice.

In other words, we simply did not leave our kids with babysitters or, really, anyone else in order to spend time away. There may have been a time or two early on that we would leave the kids with friends (who were more like family) for just a while, when it was imperative that we do something together. But I can count those times on one hand and still have fingers left over. We simply, for better or worse, decided that it was more important for us to have peace of mind with regards to whom we left our kids with than spending prolonged periods of time together alone. As a result, we did not really "do" date nights or romantic weekend getaways. That's not to cast aspersions on those who did not or do not do things the way we did them. Truth is, we missed out on some things taking this course of action. We did. But we felt that what we missed was tolerable compared to the peace of mind we gained by doing it the way we did. I'm not telling you this to give you advice on what you should do or to have you critique what you have done. It is just important, for our discussion, that you understand our mindset regarding time away with each other as a couple, in order to understand the revelation of what bonding and growing actually look like in real life.

But please don't misunderstand. I don't mean to insinuate that we neglected our marriage in favor of raising our children safely. Those two ideals are not mutually exclusive. What I do mean is that we sacrificed a bit of that aspect of our marriage, in order to ensure our children's safety and to guarantee our sanity. To be honest, we would not have been able to enjoy any potential alone time if we were constantly worried about the kids. It just would not have worked for us. However, we did take opportunities to be alone within the context we chose to live our lives. I still have very pleasant memories of bonding and growing moments we enjoyed while our kids were still little. One of the good things about having fairly young children is that they have fairly early bedtimes. More times than not, our kids were generally in bed by 8:00 pm most nights when they were quite young. That gave my bride and me opportunity to seize those moments.

One of my favorite memories from that time centers around our stay-at-home date nights. It became a pretty regular thing. I would go out and pick up some type of carry-out meal, after which we would set up the food on our kids' small activity table. We would then take out a movie we had either rented or owned, sit together at the tiny table, eat our food, and watch our movie. It didn't matter the type of food or the type of movie. It was a time where we could explore bonding and growing within the limited context we had set for our marriage. There are always opportunities for this, if we are just cognizant of those opportunities. However, I would not see how necessary this component of marriage really could be until years later, when our children were older and we were approaching the end of our time in the Navy.

As I stated at the beginning of this book, the military takes a significant toll on a family, especially as it relates to being away from the family due to operational demands, including multi-month deployments. In other words, to put it indelicately, it sucked being away from my family. We never enjoyed it. We never got used to it. It was simply a way of life that we had to incorporate into our family dynamics. To be honest, that was probably another reason why my wife and I rarely (and I mean rarely) did much apart from our kids. Because I was away from them so much in the first place, I didn't want to intentionally contribute to more separation. We were not willing to separate voluntarily as a family, due to how much time we already had to spend a part. But then something interesting happened. And it happens to every single parent on the planet. You blink your eyes, and your children are not really children anymore. Not in the strictest sense. They grow from toddling around in diapers to pre-teen and teen years in a heartbeat. It's like some kind of time-warp. In fact, it happens so fast that, many times, parents have a hard time keeping up and coming to the realization that your children now need and rely on you less and less, from a certain age onwards.

Up to this point, everything we did and every plan we made was poured through the filter of how it was going to impact the kids. Don't get me wrong, I'm not complaining about this. In fact, there are times I desperately miss it. I wouldn't have had it any other way. But there is a moment when it just sort of hits you that your kids are growing up and that their time left in your house is rapidly declining. I can tell you when that reality hit me. It happened on a Saturday morning. It doesn't matter the exact date. I probably would have a hard time telling you even what year it was. But I remember exactly how it unfolded.

We always took Saturday as a day to sleep in just a bit later than we did during the week, which included an hour drive for me to Camp Lejeune and Kimberly's preparation for that day's homeschooling lesson. By late, I mean maybe 8:30 or even 9:00, if we were feeling particularly lazy. So it was a typical Saturday morning for us that would end with things changing for us in amazing ways. We got up and began to piddle around the house, and I made a suggestion that was not out of the ordinary. I suggested to my bride that we go out for breakfast. Immediately, she agreed and started upstairs to wake the kids to go with us. I stopped her. I had a completely radical (and possibly dangerous) idea. "Let's just you and I go," I said bravely. Dare we? Should we embark on this extraordinarily ambitious and reckless journey? We should, I concluded. I don't know why it just hit me then, but our kids were not really kids anymore. One was late teens, two were later pre-teens, and all of them were smart kids. What if the house catches on fire? I was pretty sure they were old enough and smart enough to leave a burning house without us having to tell them. And by the way, all we were doing was going to the Hardee's that was exactly 4 minutes up the road. At that distance, they could call us to report the fire and we would be able to finish our breakfast, get in the car, and evacuate them ourselves (I'm, of course, kidding, but you get the point).

So we decided we would do it. We would go to Hardee's, by ourselves, and have breakfast. By ourselves. I cannot tell you what an impact this had on our marriage. I know it will sound like a little thing to you. That's why I said earlier that no one can give you a multi-step process to guarantee bonding and growing, because that will look different to each couple. We sat in that Hardee's and ate and talked and laughed and prayed and grew. With no other distractions, we focused on each other. We listened to each other. I even made sure, as best I could, that I would sit with my back to the television they had mounted in the corner, to eliminate any particular distraction. It wasn't the location or the food (that would change from week to week). It was the fact that it was just the two of us, focusing on each other and our family, even if it was just for an hour or so.

These outings were, of course, not the only time we talked about things. But there was something about having a dedicated time and place designed for one thing and one thing only: to grow and bond. That's it. So amazing was this experience that, without even discussing it, this became a weekly, Saturday ritual. There were always a few times where things would keep us from engaging in this new ritual. But we considered this time sacred. It became sacred to us. That is one of the keys to understanding the importance of growing and bonding. You absolutely have to be intentional about this time, and you need to see it as a sacred time, given up only in cases that cannot be helped. If you don't see it as sacred, you will not keep it as a priority. Let me explain how sacrosanct it became to me.

After being told by my boss that I was not going to have to deploy again (and I was stupid enough to believe that), the very same guy called me into his office to tell me I was going to have to deploy again. The chaplain scheduled to go had gotten ill and could not go, and I was next on the list. While I was not happy about this (I was never happy about leaving my family), I was a Sailor, and I immediately shifted gears to, once again, prepare to be away from my family for 6 months. This deployment would be different for me in two interesting ways. First, I was being deployed to Europe (Sicily, to be exact), which had never happened to me. Second, the timing of the deployment would ensure that I would miss Christmas with my family for the first time in my entire life. That's right. I spent 20 years in the Navy and only had one Christmas away from my family. I had missed several Thanksgivings and more birthdays and anniversaries than I can count, but I had never spent a Christmas away from home. I was not bitter (there have been a lot of people who have missed a lot of Christmases over the years), but I was a bit sad. I was always sad leaving my family, but we make a big deal about Christmas. I mean a really, really big deal about Christmas. It's all I can do to keep my wife from putting up Christmas decorations in the summer. To her, once Independence Day is over, it's time to put up the Christmas tree. I am, of course, exaggerating... but not by much.

We love Christmas at our house, and now we were about to spend our first Christmas apart. It was somber around the old Purvis house as the deployment grew near. That always happened. However, this time the pall was a bit gloomier because, even though it was summer, we were already mourning the loss of Christmas. But I made a mistake. I thought that missing Christmas was going to be the worst part about this deployment. I was wrong. After all, Christmas is just one day, right? Don't get me wrong, it's a very important day. However, it is just one day out of the entire deployment. As much as I thought I would miss and be sad about Christmas (and I was), that paled in comparison to the loneliest day I could possibly imagine, the day that I missed more than I thought possible. Can you guess what day I am referring to? Yep, Saturday. Specifically, Saturday mornings.

The loneliness pangs I felt while on that deployment were ratcheted up to the extreme on Saturday mornings. I missed my wife more on those Saturday mornings than I did Christmas morning. I'm going to be honest — I didn't think that was possible. Yet, there I was. I never felt more like was on deployment than on that day. It was an emptiness I cannot explain even now. Why? Because the sacred had been stripped from me. That almost holy time with my wife (at a Hardee's, of all places) was missing. And when the sacred is ripped from you, you feel it in ways you couldn't have possibly imagined. Oh, we did the best we could with it. I would sleep as late as I could possibly make myself sleep before I would head over to the base food court. I would order a pizza, take my Bible and read it a bit, and then text with Kimberly for a bit while I was sitting there. Even though it was early (very early) for her when we would start, she never missed a moment of trying to recover what little bit of sacred we could from that time.

Again, that's why I say that it would be a fool's game for me to try and tell you what growing and bonding you should be engaging in. But I hope you see that it has nothing too much to do with location or activity. It has everything to do with discovering that thing that allows you to focus on each other in a way that keeps distractions to a minimum. It has everything to do with finding a time that is considered sacred, sacrosanct, hallowed, revered, or however you want to describe it. It has to be noticeable when you miss it. In fact, I believe it has to hurt a little to miss it. If it doesn't hurt to miss it, how sacred can it actually be? I wish I could just give you a list of activities that you can engage in that would be considered effective bonding. But that would mean that I know what you consider sacred. I will say this: though this endeavor might be difficult to define, you will know it when you see it. Or, more accurately, you'll know it when you feel it. So it's not a matter of me telling you to simply do A, B, and C and you will be bonding and growing. I just want to share with you enough so that you know it when you see and feel it.

Calculatus Eliminatus.

If you're not familiar with the faux Latin term above, it is from one of my all-time favorite cartoons, released in 1971 and loved by millions, including me. The cartoon I'm talking about is the animated feature, *The Cat in the Hat*, which was modeled after the famous Dr. Seuss book of the same name. If you're not familiar with the television adaptation of the story, the plot revolves around a 6-foot tall cat who inserts himself into the quiet lives of two children who had been left home alone while their mother ran some errands. Since it was a rainy day, the obviously free-range kids were sequestered in the house with little to nothing to do. Hence, the Cat. He bursts in uninvited to assure the kids that, even though they cannot enjoy outside activities because of the rain, he was there to make sure they had fun inside the house. Though there is a problem.

Apparently, the mother had given the children very sound and logical advice to not allow anyone in the house while she was gone. The Cat, who did not seem phased by this reality, engages in somewhat obnoxious behavior that seems a bit off-putting to say the least. The family goldfish (you really have to see this, in order for it to make sense) admonishes the Cat to leave immediately, while constantly reminding everyone that the mother would not like this talking, hatted feline in their home. Dejected, but accepting of his fate, the Cat leaves the house only to immediately return. The reason for his return? He had lost his "moss-covered three-handled family gradunza" and he was not leaving until he found it. But since the Cat (inexplicably) could not describe the item, he implemented a search procedure to find it. He called it: Calculatus Eliminatus.

The idea behind this ridiculous name is actually very logically sound. The Cat suggested they check and then mark and rule out every spot the item was *not* found. In doing so, by eliminating the other options, they would eventually find what they were looking for. In his own words: "The way to find a missing something is to find out where it's not." Again, all the Cat was suggesting was process of elimination. The idea behind this is that every failure will simply draw us to the ultimate success. Legend has it that Thomas Edison tried 100 different iterations of the lightbulb before finding success. When asked, so the legend goes, how it felt to fail 100 times, Edison insisted he never failed once. He was alleged to have said, "I just found 100 ways how *not* to make a lightbulb." The insinuation is that every failure will make the ultimate success that much more findable.

Now, I realize this is a long way to go to make an example related to discovering what bonding and growing actually is, but bear with me. As I stated earlier, it is extremely difficult to quantitatively define what growing and bonding is in such a way that it applies to everyone. Some people will look at my story about breakfasts at Hardee's as being the most lame attempt at bonding they have ever heard of. For me, it was life-changing. We have different life-filters related to our personality, our like/ dislikes, and what will work for us. This entire idea has an element of pragmatism that rightfully exposes the reality that, what works as bonding for one person, may not work for another. Since that is the case, I decided to take a bit of advice from the Cat in the Hat. If the key to finding something is to find out where it is not, then certainly one of the best ways to understand what something *is*, is to examine what it is *not*. In other words, for our purpose, one of the best ways to evaluate what good, effective, solid bonding and growing is, is to identify those things that will keep it from happening. Make any sense? I may not be able to give you a list of activities guaranteed to foster growing and bonding. What I can (and will) do is provide you with a list of activities that have, in my vast experience, the likelihood of ensuring that bonding will not take place. These are the enemies of bonding, the parasites that drain the lifeblood of growing and bonding. I hope that, by seeing these, you will be that much closer to seeing what bonding and growing actually looks like in your own unique situation. So let's take a look at the things that distract us from the growing and bonding we must engage in, so that we can have the optimal marriage God has for us.

Jobs. This is a significant one. First, my disclaimer. There is nothing wrong with having a job you love and want to do well in.

There is a very well-known leadership and management theory referred to as Theory X and Theory Y, developed by a man named Douglas McGregor. The idea behind this approach is revealed via its simple brilliance. McGregor suggests that every leader is either a Theory X leader or a Theory Y leader. Simply put, a Theory X leader believes that people inherently dislike work, are not inherently motivated to work hard, and thus will try to find ways to avoid working. This drives the Theory X leader to engage leadership techniques that are harsh, dictatorial, and controlling, in order to accomplish the goals of the organization. Theory Y leaders, on the other hand, are folks that believe people enjoy their work, are intrinsically endowed (for the most part) with the desire to do well, and are motivated to do a good job. As a result, the Theory Y leader will employ a management and motivational style different from their Theory X counterparts. Theory Y leaders are more inspirational, they engage in less micromanaging, and will not typically engage threats to accomplish the mission of the organization. Now, these are very gross oversimplifications of these approaches, but this is not a book about leadership. I only bring it up because I fall firmly into the camp of a Theory Y leader. I think people are fulfilled by their job. And, in and of itself, that is not necessarily a bad thing. Working ensures we take care of our family and can provide them the basic necessities of life, along with some creature comforts as well. Plus, it allows us to be a part of something bigger than ourselves and to build something of substance. However, that is not what I am talking about.

What I am talking about is allowing your work to determine something that work was *never* designed to determine: your identity. I have seen it over and over and over again. Time after time, I have seen people mistakenly believe that their work defines who they are as a human being. Nothing could be further from the truth. I have been telling people this for years: work is what you *do*, it is not who you *are*. If we do not get this right, work will then become the thing we will grow and bond with. The old adage is true — nobody's tombstone ever says, "I wish I had spent more time at the office." Old adages are old for a reason; they have been proven true over and again. Please, do not misunderstand. I am not telling you to not work hard. I am not telling you to not enjoy your work. I am not telling you to eschew upward advancement. I am telling you to keep these things in the perspective in which it was designed.

In Genesis, as God was creating the world and everything in it, He saved His greatest creation (humans) for last. Throughout the creative process, the writer of Genesis uses the same phrase over and over again. In fact, this phrase was used seven times to describe the ultimate value of the creation process. Genesis records seven times that God looked at His creation and "saw that it was good" (Genesis 1:4, 10, 18, 20, 25, 31). This was God's way of letting us know the value He placed on the world He created and how important it is for us to understand this. It also seems abundantly clear that He was using this phrase to illustrate another, even more important, aspect of humanity, discussed in Chapter two of Genesis. After telling us over and over again that what He created and saw was "good," He then reveals something to us that was "not good." The something that was not good? "It is not good that man should be alone" (Genesis 2:18). I can't tell you how important this statement is for a variety of reasons, not the least of which pertains to our subject here.

First of all, Adam was not "technically" alone. "The Lord God formed every beast of the field and every bird of the air, and brought them to Adam to see what he called them" (Genesis 2:19). Adam was surrounded by animals and was entrenched in a perfect world. But it was not enough. God clearly articulated that it was not good for Adam to be alone. The animals and his surroundings were not enough. God didn't create a brother or sister or aunt or uncle for Adam to assuage his loneliness. He didn't create a never-ending series of works for Adam to engage in to "keep him busy" and, therefore, eliminate this loneliness. Instead, He created a family for Adam. He created a wife for Adam. It was the wife that would fulfill Adam ultimately, with regards to his loneliness and his purpose. Adam had an entire world at his disposal. With enough work to last multiple lifetimes. But God knew that Adam would not find fulfillment in that work. He would find personal fulfillment in his relationship with his wife.

This has not changed. Sure, the introduction of sin has corrupted this ideal, as it has corrupted everything it touches. But it has not changed the intent to have our relationship with our wife supersede our relationship with our work. Work is a good thing. When it becomes an idol, an end instead of a means to an end, it becomes a very bad thing. Because it will directly impede our ability to grow and bond with our spouse. It just will. I wish I could tell you differently, but I can't. Your job should be important to you. But never more important than your spouse. That doesn't mean you will never do difficult things as a part of that job that will affect your relationship with your wife. I married my wife and had kids so I could spend more time with them, not less. Yet for 20 years, I worked at a job that cause me to spend months and months away from my family. But here's the thing. They always knew that I didn't want to go. They knew, as I knew, that it was simply part of the job that God had called me to. They knew how much it crushed me to be away from them. They knew that they were my priority, even when I was half a world away for months at a time. May I show you the difference between this and putting your job first?

I met a Navy Chaplain some years ago. For confidentiality reasons, we will simply call him Bob (not his real name) . Not that he wasn't a nice guy. He was just completely obtuse about this subject. People liked him, and he was (I assume still is) a very engaging person. He had one relationally fatal flaw that became apparent about three minutes after you met him. His job as a Navy Chaplain meant more to him than his family. I know that sounds judgmental, but it's not. I am merely making an observation. I will concede that referring to him in this way does carry some judgmental connotations, but I just call 'em like I see 'em. It wasn't long after I met him that my initial suspicions concerning his family taking a backseat to his job was confirmed. It would be difficult to go into specifics without describing details that might inevitably identify this person, but let me put it like this.

One of the goals of many Navy chaplains is to reach the highest rank they can achieve. For many, that is the rank of 0-6, or Captain (to be differentiated from the other services, whose 0-6 rank is called Colonel). I never cared because I was never going to spend one day past 20 years in the first place. In fact, I never thought I would be in the Navy for that long anyway. But this Captain thing means a lot to plenty of people. It especially meant a lot to Bob. So much so that he did everything he thought he needed to do, job-wise, in order to assure his eventual promotion to Captain, which included volunteering for assignments he felt would make him look better for promotion but would also ensure he spent a tremendous amount of time away from his family. Note, he did not have to take these jobs. They were not a part of the normal cycle of operational and then non-operational assignments that plays out in the life of a military member. He went out of his way to take jobs that were not a part of the "normal" rotation of deployments and that, in fact, included time away from his family that he did not have to endure. His thought had to have been, "I'll take these difficult assignments, which will separate me from my family, in order to show the Navy how valuable I am to them so they will promote me." It worked. And along the way, he also lost his family.

I knew this guy. I knew his family. I could never have imagined his wife would be the type to seek the solace of someone else outside her relationship with her husband. Getting to know the wife, I would have *never* gotten the idea that it could have been possible for her to engage in an extramarital relationship. But she did. I am not excusing what she did. Please do not hear me say this. What I am saying is that, while her husband was busy bonding and growing with this job (his true love), she was bonding and growing with someone else. She was to blame for this. He was to blame for this. By the way, there is proof that he recognized this as well. Years later, he was serving with a friend of mine, and an interesting thing happened. On his first attempt at promotion to Captain, he was not selected. He was devastated. My friend and I were talking about this situation one day, and he told me how Bob responded when he found out he was not selected the first time (he was subsequently selected his second time around). My friend told me that Bob said to him, "And look what I gave up to get this."

Interesting, isn't it? By the time he was in place for selection to Captain, his wife and their kids had already left him. They were the price for his idolization of his job. He was actually acknowledging that he had sacrificed his family for a rank. Think about that for a moment. And ask yourself if you are doing the same thing. Don't get me wrong, I am not saying that Bob's pursuit of his career was the only thing that sent his wife into the arms of another. Things like this are always way more complicated than that. However, his actions made it clear that he had chosen to bond with his job over bonding with his wife. And there is always a price to pay for that. God did not create us exclusively to have a career. He said it was not good that Adam was alone, and so He created a wife. That is our primary focus. Note, I did not say our only focus. We can focus on a lot of important things. But we are talking about things that rob us of our ability to grow and bond with our spouse. And if we do not grow and bond with our spouse, we will never have the optimal marriage God intends for us. So the question we have to ask is: am I letting my job define me, or am I letting my role as spouse define me? Are you better at your job than you are as a husband or wife? If so, that is a fatal problem.

Other relationships. I know this is a very broad term, so let me try and narrow it down just a bit. And let me begin that narrowing process by clarifying something that I believe is very important. When I discuss that "outside" relationships can rob us of the time, energy, and inclination to bond and grow with our spouse, I include the same caveat from the previous discussion about jobs. These things are a danger to our desire and ability to bond with our spouse if we allow ourselves to lose perspective. If these extramarital relationships (and I don't mean that necessarily as a negative) become more relational to us than bonding with our spouse, that will be a significant problem and a significant barrier to marital bonding and growing. Let me also provide another disclaimer. I am not in any way, shape, or form suggesting that married individuals should not have close, meaningful relationships outside of their marriage. Not at all. What I *am* saying is that, if these relationships in any way take the place of relational aspects which are supposed to be held by the spouse, these other relationships become parasitic in your quest to bond with your spouse.

We've all seen (at least, I assume that we have) stories told via sitcoms, movies, and even cartoons of the married couple where things get so bad that the wife will usually threaten to go "back home to mother." It is a very cliché device used over and again, but it does bring up an interesting foundational issue. If we can agree that there is such a thing as a relationship that is extramarital (again, here I am using this term to simply mean a relationship with a person who is not your spouse; in this context, even a relationship with your children is technically extramarital) which can possibly sabotage our attempts at bonding with our spouse, what do these relationships look like? The short answer is: they can look like almost anything, including extended family.

Hear me out. I am not saying that married couples cannot or should not have a very close relationship with their extended family, especially their parents. That assertion would not only be untrue and preposterous but also unbiblical. When God proclaimed the ten most important commandments He could assert to help guide His people, He included only one that had a promise associated with it. The 5th Commandment states, "Honor your father and mother, that your days may be long upon the land" (Exodus 20:12). It is crystal clear that God obviously wants us to continue to have a very close and respectful relationship with our parents. This ideal is reinforced in many places throughout Scripture. However, He does not want that relationship to ever become more important than our relationship with our spouse. How do I know this? How can I make such a claim? Again, because God told us this when He created the institution of marriage in the first place. After God created Eve, God states clearly, "Therefore, a man shall *leave his mother and father* [italics mine] and be joined to his wife, and they shall become one flesh" (Genesis 2:24). We are not to be one flesh with our parents, our siblings, our aunts/uncles, or our cousins. There is only one person on the planet we are to bond and grow with to the point where we become one. That is our spouse. In the King James Version of the Bible, it reads that, as spouses, we are to "leave" and "cleave". That is, leave our parents and cleave to one another.

The marital relationship is the preeminent human relationship we are to have on this planet. Of course, our relationship with God comes before all others, which is supported throughout Scripture. But when it comes to interpersonal human relationships, there is not one that will top the marriage relationship. Remember what I said earlier. If we do not heed the instructions of the Designer of marriage, we cannot have the marriage He designed us to have. Yes, of course our blood relatives are to be a continuous, vital, important part of our lives once we are married. But if I were forced to choose between my blood relatives and my bride, I would not even have to think about it. My bride and I are one. That is the way marriage should be viewed. Imagine how many fewer divorces would take place today if people really viewed marriage in this way.

This does not mean that we cannot seek out the counsel of our parents, even about our marriage. They can be a source of great insight when it comes to the ins and outs of navigating marital waters. However, if the issues you discuss with your parents never then are raised with your spouse, that could be a problem. It simply means that you are releasing frustrations about your spouse to an obviously sympathetic ear but not really addressing the one who can actually do anything about it. You may be bonding with your parent, but you certainly are not bonding with your spouse. And it is vitally important that you bond with your spouse; not so much with your parents. By the time you are at this point, you've had decades to bond with your parents. It is now time to grow with the person with whom you've become one. May I, again, give you an example of this?

Many years ago, we had a dear friend who married a man that she loved but was probably not a very good fit for her. One of the more interesting aspects of this relationship was that her husband was really and truly a "mama's boy." Note that many times this is used as a badge of honor, while other times it is seen as a pejorative. The truth is somewhere in between. But in this case, it was a gigantic problem. He spoke to his mother about things he should have shared with his wife. He took his mother's plans into consideration, rather than his wife's. One of the proverbial straws came when the young wife was in their apartment alone and heard the front door opening. A bit frightened, she walked into the main room to see her mother-in-law opening the front door of the apartment with her own key. Her son had given her the key, not for emergency purposes as some people are wont to do, but so she could have unfettered access to the apartment any time she wished. See, this is a problem. The husband continued to bond with his mother while relegating his wife to a distant second. It would be an oversimplification to suggest that this was the only reason their marriage ended. But it would be equally misleading to suggest that this had very little to do with it. The husband's lack of bonding and growing with his wife was a major contributor to their failed marriage. That relationship became a parasite designed to drain the lifeblood from the growing that should have been taking place between a husband and a wife. We have to be careful. Love your parents and your family. Embrace their love. Seek their advice, and enjoy being with them. But grow with your spouse. Bond with them. Become one with them.

Unfortunately, relatives are not the only potentially parasitic relationships that can corrupt our desires and opportunities to grow and bond with our spouse. As the years went on in my counseling sessions, I began to notice a troubling trend. I was seeing more and more married people who had developed very close relationships with friends who just happened to be the opposite sex. Simply put, this is a problem. Note that I am trying not to be an alarmist here, nor am I painting with an infinite-sized brush. It would be the height of foolishness to make a statement so broad in its scope that it would be immediately dismissed for its hyper-hyperbole. A mistake like that would then lead any serious-minded person to automatically reject any conclusions drawn from that exaggeration without any pause to determine the possible veracity of the claim. I could follow up an outrageous statement with solid advice, only to have that advice immediately dismissed because it would have occurred under the umbrella of the outrageous statement. Make any sense? So I want to be careful not to understate or overstate this next extremely important point. The point is this: no married person should have a deep, ongoing, devoted friendship with a member of the opposite sex.

Notice, I did not say that men and women cannot be friends. I did not say that married men and married women cannot be friends with members of the opposite sex. I did not say that married men and women cannot speak to, laugh with, and have serious discussions with members of the opposite sex. What I did say is that, if you are married and you are having a deep, personal, ongoing, and devoted relationship with a person of the opposite sex that is not your spouse, that is a serious problem. In fact, it is (or will be) a *very* serious problem. Please understand what I am trying to say, and know that I am saying this not because someone told me about it, or I read about it, or I studied it in a book, but because I have seen this arise over and over again. I have never personally ever seen a situation where this works out and everyone is happy about it. That's not to say that situation doesn't exist. I am just saying that, in the hundreds of couples I have spoken to, I have never, ever, not once had a spouse say to me, "I'm so glad my husband (or wife) has another member of the opposite sex with whom they can confide and have deep, meaningful conversations." There may be some who say it doesn't bother them (which I don't ever believe), but I have never heard a spouse laud and commend their spouse, their "one flesh" partner, for having a meaningful relationship with a member of the opposite sex. There is a good reason for that.

Remember, we are talking about what it means to bind with your spouse and what parasites are out there ready to drain the lifeblood from that process. If the marriage relationship is more binding and more devotional in nature than even the relationship between a parent and a child (and according to Genesis 2:24, it is), then how much more is the marital relationship compared to any friendship, especially a friendship with a member of the opposite sex. Ongoing, close, devoted, meaningful friendships with members of the opposite sex guarantees two things. One, it guarantees you will talk to this person about things that you and your spouse talk about. Which is not good. Two, it guarantees you will talk to that person about things you and your spouse *don't* talk about. And that is way worse. It is inevitable. You will have discussions with this person about things concerning your life, your marriage, and your spouse that you will never say to your spouse. It will happen every single time. You will justify it, of course. You will say, "This is a way to get a guy's (or girl's) perspective on this (whatever 'this' is)." So no harm done. But you don't need a guy or girl's perspective on this. You need your spouse's perspective on this. That's what bonding is all about. And the more personal and intimate the conversation is with the friend of the opposite sex, the further down the road you are to distancing yourself from your spouse. Oh, you will do a great job of bonding — with the friend. That's what happens when you have conversations with someone that you don't have with anyone else. You form a bond. You are bonding with the friend and not your spouse. I implore you, with all that is within me, spend that time talking and bonding with your spouse, and don't let a "friendship" become parasitic to that endeavor.

Privacy. I have to say that, of all of the parasites out there that are designed to derail the bonding between husband and wife, this is the one that is the most ridiculous. I know the nuances and manifestations of this idea are more understandable, but the basis of this one just escapes me. In fact, I would often find myself listening to a counselee trying to explain this idea in a rational way, only to have to fight the urge to holler out, "That's the stupidest thing I've ever heard of." Which is generally a frowned-upon counseling tactic. I know where the incredulity about this subject started for me. Prior to joining the Navy, I was a member of the South Carolina Army National Guard. I joined both to serve my state and nation, as well as to earn money for college. Both admirable reasons to join. And I was able to accomplish all of those things. In fact, my unit was called to active duty in support of Operation Desert Storm. So all together, I actually served 26 years in the military. Man, when you say it out loud like that, you really feel the weight of what it means to spend half your life associated with the military. Anyway, while I served in the National Guard I, of course, got to meet a lot of good folks who floated in and out of the unit. There was one guy in particular that I really liked and respected. I was not married at the time but was dating my future wife. If I had to guess, I would surmise that this guy would have been married about 10 years or so, maybe a bit more.

In one conversation, I heard him mention that he had left his job and was heading to a new one. He also said that he would be between jobs for a few weeks while waiting for the new one to start. He began to lament the fact that he would go about two weeks without getting a paycheck and how it was coming at a bad time with some bills to be paid. Then he said something really interesting. He told me he was going to have to borrow some money from his wife. This sounded foreign to me. After all, you *borrow* money from others. You *borrow* money from banks. Do you really *borrow* money from your spouse? How does that work? Do you sign paperwork? Is there an IOU? What about interest or closing costs? I was taken aback by this verbiage, which seemed very impersonal and a bit selfish to me. I mean, isn't sharing what marriage is about? Remember, I was not married but would be before I left the Guard. So I was like a sponge during this time, trying to get as much solid advice about marriage as I could before I took the plunge. So I asked what he meant by borrowing money from his wife. To me, the tale got even stranger.

He told me that he and his wife both had jobs (ok, sounds normal so far) and that they also had their own bank accounts (ok, not so normal anymore). They viewed the money they made as their own money in their own accounts to do with what they wanted. They divided the bills (I have no idea how that worked) and what was left over was theirs and theirs alone. Unless, of course, they found it in their generous hearts to lend money to their spouse in case of emergency. Let me stop here a minute. I am not saying that this arrangement is inherently *wrong*. Not at all. I have heard of other folks doing this, though I must admit that it is one of the weirdest things I have ever heard of. It was weird to me then, it is weird to me now. But hey, weird things work all the time, so who knows. But I just couldn't get past this whole thing with my friend. Even before I was married, I had this crazy idea that we were both in it together. I never thought in terms of hers/mine about anything, especially money. I don't know, it always seemed to me that keeping a separate account and thinking of some money as "mine" and not "hers" always smacked of mistrust. Before you bring out the pitchforks, let me say this again. If you are reading this and that is the way you and your spouse are doing this, I am not saying you do not trust each other. I said that is the way *I* would feel. I mean, if my bride and I share each other's bodies, sharing money sort of seems like a given. The whole thing sort of seemed like an unnecessary desire for a level of privacy that I don't need to have from my wife.

In the culture in which we live today, especially with the advent of social media, privacy is a very big deal. We need to know about and be wary of people or entities (Google and Facebook, I'm looking at you) who want unfettered access to our privacy. In my view, we as a culture are way too willing to sign away our right to privacy. There are plenty of people, businesses, and governments we need to be wary of when it comes to our privacy. I will say this, though, loud and clear and with no qualification: we do not need to do this with our spouse. If you want to make an argument for protection from an invasion of privacy, your spouse should *never* (under normal circumstances) be the subject of that argument. I have seen this over and over and over again. And the rise in these instances have been commensurate with the advent and rise of social media and gadgets (phones, tablets, watches, etc). I remember early in my career how extremely rare it was for me to do premarital counseling with a couple who had met "online." And it was equally odd for them, as many of them would tell me this almost sheepishly. By the end of my career, it was extremely commonplace for people to have connected or reconnected online via dating sites or (way more often) social media sites (specifically Facebook). And as technology has made it easier and easier to connect with people all over the world, it has also created a ton of unintended consequences.

I maintain that the more we have become connected electronically, the less connected we have become personally. We have "friends" who are anything but and "followers" despite the fact that we don't lead. This is a book on marriage, however, so I am more interested here in revealing the parasites that will keep you from growing and bonding in the way God intended than to lament our electronically induced cultural malaise. Remember, we are talking about the idea of privacy in a marriage relationship and how parasitic that can be. And this problem is exacerbated by the emergence of social media. Allow me to elaborate.

One of the more unavoidable privacy-related aspects to our gadgets and our social media is the necessity for passwords. Think about it. Almost everything we engage with has a password related to it in some way, shape, or form. And I know you know this, but passwords are designed to keep people out of your phones, tablets, computers, Facebook pages, Instagram pages, email — in other words, everything. Since we are (for good or bad) in this technological reality for the long haul, passwords are and will remain a vital part of protecting our privacy. *But not from our spouse!* Here is where it morphs from necessary reality to marriage parasite. Because, I don't know if you've noticed it or not, but for all the good that a site like Facebook has done (and I believe it has), there is also a bucketload of bad. I will wager that there is not one person reading this right now who has not personally known, or heard of, someone's marriage relationship being destroyed by connecting or reconnecting with someone on Facebook. Do not misunderstand, I am not blaming Mark Zuckerberg for this. He did not invent sin. He just invented a platform to make sin easier. Facebook is a thing, neither good nor bad. It is our predilection for sin that takes a "thing" and uses it for bad. Facebook has been used for bad. A lot of bad. I have seen marriage after marriage fall apart because of someone's misuse of social media. I'm using Facebook here as the face of all social media. I do not intend to single only them out or let the others off the hook. And one of the reasons these gadgets and platforms are so adept at being used this way is, in part, because you need a password to get into them.

Some years ago, I was counseling a couple in severe distress. It seemed the husband had been having ongoing personal conversations (a previous parasite we discussed earlier) with an old girlfriend via social media. They had reconnected by way of Facebook. Sound familiar? I wish I had a dime for every couple I counseled in this area. I'm sure it probably started out very innocently. I am also sure the conversation began to devolve relatively quickly and became more personal and more intimate over time. You want to know why? Because the husband did not have to worry about his wife accidentally stumbling across this conversation. You want to know why? Because she didn't have the password. There was absolutely no accountability in this conversation in any way, shape, or form. His parasite was password-protected. He knew she could not stumble across this conversation. What he didn't count on was the fact that she might want to intentionally try to discover the conversation. Which is exactly what she wanted to do and what she did. Sensing something was amiss, she set out to try and figure out the password to his Facebook account. She succeeded. As they were sitting in my office with me, revealing to me the very inappropriate conversations he was having with this old flame, do you want to know the crux of his argument?

You got it. He was complaining that she had endeavored to get into his "private" Facebook account. Oh, he paid lip service to the inappropriate conversations and acknowledged they were wrong to have. But he was way more interested in his wife's "hacking" into his account (a classic "straw man" in logic circles). I asked him why this bothered him so much, considering that maybe her doing this might have kept this from escalating to a point of no return. He answered very clearly and concisely that it was a privacy issue. A privacy issue? He had used this "privacy" to engage in inappropriate conversations with another woman and now he wanted to plant his flag on the privacy island? It was a fascinating conversation to say the least. I asked him if the privacy issue was more important than the fact that he had engaged in behavior that could have led to the ending of his relationship. He had to acknowledge that it was not. So I gave to him the same advice I have given, and continue to give, every single married and pre-married couple I have spoken to: if you have anything password-protected from your spouse, that is a *huge* problem.

It grieves me to tell you how many people then begin to argue with me about that advice. Over and again I have had one or both members of the couple try to argue with me about the positives of having passwords unknown to their spouse. I know that they're thinking. I'm the old guy from back in the stone age, and I just don't understand how gadgets and social media works. I admit that this is the case. I'm not a Luddite, but I am a sympathizer. I don't know how gadgets work all the time. I still have to ask questions about how Facebook and Twitter work. I'll be completely honest — I don't even know what Instagram is. But I know this: nobody on the planet can give me one good reason why their gadgets and their social media sites have to be password-protected from their spouse. Notice I did not say that people cannot and have not given me reasons for this. I said nobody can give me a *good* reason for this. I've heard plenty of reasons but not one good reason. I just don't get it.

With your spouse, you share your bathroom, your shower, your body, your bodily fluids (I know, but I'm trying to make a point), and your... *everything*. But you're going to try and tell me that you need not share your password with your spouse? Every time I would get a person who would want to argue with me about this, I always asked the same question: "What good does this do?" What good can come from protecting your stuff with passwords that your spouse does not know? The best they can do is to come up with things that may not hurt, but they have never come up with a reason that can be looked at as good or helpful. And is that what

117

we want as a litmus test for our marriage? Do we want to knowingly engage in activities that "may not hurt" the marriage? Don't we want to engage in activities that are "good" for the marriage? Sharing passwords with our spouse is good for marriage. It is. It subverts so many possible traps that lay in wait for us as we travail the often hazardous landscape of marriage. It is a good thing. The *best* you could hope for by keeping passwords from your spouse is that *maybe* it will do no harm. Is that what we want? Simply to do no harm? Or do we want to take positive steps to make sure the desire for "privacy" in a marriage relationship doesn't become a parasite by allowing us to engage in activities that will keep us from bonding with our spouse and keep us stuck at the bottom of the pyramid?

Why do you think I'm emphasizing this so much? Because I am immune from any of these things? If I were immune to this, if I were so "good" at this that I can give all of this great advice, then why does my wife have all of my passwords? She does, you know. And not because of some noble, empty gesture so that I can't be accused of admonishing people to do as I say and not as I do. My wife has all of my passwords because I know I can be tempted. How do I know that? Because I am a human being. I am a Believer, no longer a slave to sin (Romans 6:17-18). I have the righteousness of Christ bestowed upon me because of His sacrifice (Romans 3:21-24). I have been adopted as a child of God through Christ (Romans 8:14-17). All of these things are true. What is also true is that I still struggle with sin (Romans 7:15-20) and will until I draw my last breath on this planet and awake in the paradise of Heaven (Revelation 21:1-27). I need my wife to have access to everything I have and everything I am. If I am weak enough to do things that could harm or end my marriage (and we are all weak enough to do that), then I desperately need her to see those things. The Bible constantly warns about things done in darkness, in order for them to be hidden (John 3:19-21). Giving passwords to my wife is an amazing and trusting way for light to be shined on my deeds. We share one Facebook account. I have a "ministry" account as well. She has that password. I have an iPhone. She has that password. We share an email account, and she has access to my other ministry accounts. She has access to my entire life, every bit of it. And I wouldn't have it any other way.

Concluding thoughts.

Everything I have is hers. Every dime I make is hers. Every fear I have is hers. Every success I experience is hers. Every sorrow I feel is hers. Every joy I enjoy is hers. Privacy? From my wife? It is as foreign to me as Mandarin Chinese. I want to bond and grow with my wife. If I am not able to bond and grow with my wife, I will never, ever become one with her in the manner God has intended for us. If I am not aware of the parasites that exist that will keep me from doing that, they will do what parasites do. They will drain the lifeblood from my marriage. I have left so many things out that fall into these categories, but time is of the essence here. Things like pornography, distracting hobbies, video games (this comes up a lot), a predisposition to stuff, etc all fall under the categories we have discussed in this chapter. To be honest, we could probably narrow our entire focus to this subject of the barriers to bonding and growing and fill up a 300-page book. But how many of us are going to read a 300-page marriage book? So it's time to move on.

However, let me finish this section by, once again, trying to manage expectations. Remember how we started. There is no way I can give you a list of what bonding and growing activities looks like. People are simply too different in their likes/dislikes and wants/desires. As I stated earlier, some will look at my Saturday breakfast story and be inspired, while others will simply chalk it up to a lack of bonding creativity. But it meant (and still means) the world to Kimberly and I. Find those things you like to do. And do those things your spouse likes to do. If every single spouse would dedicate themselves to their spouse's well-being, then no need would go unfulfilled. Seems simple, but I know it can be very difficult at times. And while I cannot give you a "bonding list," what I can do (and, in fact, did) is give you a partial list of the parasites that can distract and detract from your ability to bond and grow as a couple. Remember, the Marriage Pyramid is a schematic that represents foundational marriage elements that must be in place in order for us to have the marriage God intended us to have. In other words, to have the optimal marriage possible, all things considered. So if I can't give you a list of bonding and growing things to do, I can do the next best thing: give you a list of things guaranteed to ensure that you will not grow and will not bond. I owe you that much. Because not growing and not bonding with your spouse is tragic and heartbreaking. And it will guarantee that you will never reach the final level of the Pyramid, the goal of becoming one. Let's talk about what that looks like right now.

Chapter Five
ONE

Operationalizing our constructs.

I know I talked some about this earlier, but now that we are reaching the nexus of the Marriage Pyramid, I am going to need to hearken back to some of the points I made at the beginning of the book. I will not re-hash them in detail, but I will remind us of them so I can illustrate how these things play a role in us either being able to or being thwarted from becoming one with our spouse. Because that is (as the Pyramid implies) the ultimate goal and highest state a marriage can exist in. If bonding and growing together is the penultimate goal, then becoming one is, by far, the ultimate state of being. But we have a problem. What does it mean to become one? How does that work? What does it look like? What are the steps we need to engage in to make that a reality? Those are very sound and rational questions. I'm not completely sure there is a satisfactory answer for each one. Let me use a sort of weird analogy that may not do much more than continue to muddy the waters.

Back in the 1970s, the United States Supreme Court was dealing with a very interesting and important ruling regarding the 1st Amendment and the production and dissemination of pornography. As a culture, we are still dealing with the ramifications of that discussion some 40 years after the fact. The question before the court went something like this: was the production and dissemination of pornography a crime, or was it protected under the 1st Amendment? The court issued an interesting decision. Ultimately, they decided that pornography was protected under the 1st Amendment, but obscenity was not likewise protected. Here's the fascinating part. The court did not define the difference between the two. When one Justice was asked about the difference between obscenity and pornography, he uttered the now-famous reply, "I may not be able to define it, but I know it when I see it." Amazing that this is a person who is supposed to be so precise with legal language, and yet this was the best he could do in answer to a very logical, rational question. What in the world does this story have to do with the discussion of what it means to become one with our spouse?

Simply, it means that though I may have a difficult time defining that principle, I know becoming one when I see it. Here is the caveat though. I see it only by way of viewing it through the prism of God's Word. I don't know it because I see it based on the world's view of becoming one (in whatever form that may be). I know it. I recognize it because of what God tells me I am to look for with regards to this entire idea. Remember, marriage was the very first institution God ever created. It predates the creation of the church. When God saw that it was not good that Adam was alone, He did not create a dog, horse, or hamster for him. He created Eve and performed the very first marriage ceremony in history. And within that ceremony, He very clearly states, "A man shall leave his father and mother and be joined to his wife, and they shall become one flesh" (Genesis 2:24 NKJV). So there we see plainly that this idea of becoming one is not verbiage that I came up with but is verbiage that the God of the universe spoke in conjunction with His ideal of marriage. But once again I will ask the questions. What does that mean? What does it look like? How does it work? To even try to answer some of these questions, we have to stay with the source. Let's take a look at the two obvious meanings behind this statement.

Sex. First, He is clearly referencing the idea of sexual intercourse as being a part of this idea of becoming one. The use of the phrase "become one flesh" is very telling here as it relates to this idea. God makes it very clear that the act of sexual intercourse is vital to the idea of marriage in general and to the idea of becoming one specifically. The way our bodies are designed for heterosexual sex illustrates this wonderful idea that, while we are engaged in that sacred act (and that is exactly what it was intended to be), it is nearly impossible to tell where the flesh from one starts and the flesh of the other ends. It is an amazing, real-life picture of the words God used to explain the preciousness of this act in conjunction with the sacredness of the institution. And think about it — if God had wanted to, He could have made procreation a non-pleasurable, perfunctory task simply designed to ensure the survival of the species. Yet, He did the exact opposite. He designed sexual intercourse as the single most intimate, pleasurable experience two people can share together.

If you're unsure of any of this, please just go read Song of Solomon. There are people (including some Believers) who are convinced God created sex exclusively as a way to procreate. That is certainly a huge part of it (Genesis 1:28). However, when one peruses the pages of the Song of Solomon, we see a husband and wife who rejoice in each other's bodies from a sexual standpoint, including acts and parts of the body that have nothing to do with procreation. Sex was God's wonderful gift within the context of His first institution. God designed this physical, intimate act to be a picture of what marriage was supposed to be and was intended for. And when you look at how this is manifested throughout Scripture, you then have a better understanding of what is meant in other passages about this subject.

In the Sermon on the Mount, Jesus states that anyone who marries a woman who is divorced "commits adultery" (Matthew 5:32b). Today, we might view a statement like this as being overly critical or unnecessarily harsh. Looking at it this way misses the point. This passage is simply stating that, even if you are culturally divorced, as far as God is concerned you are still married. And if you are still married, then you must only have sex with *that*. If you marry a person, you will have sex with them. So if you have sex with a person who is divorced (and still married to their partner, in the eyes of God), then you are engaging in an act meant only for your spouse. Likewise, you will not be able to become one with that person because you can only become one with your spouse. And in the eyes of God, that person you divorced is still your spouse. People make the mistake of thinking this passage is about divorce. It's not. This passage is telling us clearly what it means to become one flesh. And you cannot become one with anyone who is not your spouse. That is obviously a view of sex our culture has incrementally ignored, much to our detriment.

Think of how many heartaches, diseases, social calamities, and family dysfunctions could be avoided if we viewed sex in the sacred manner in which God designed it. Extraordinary, isn't it? Instead, our culture insists that sex is not sacred and should be experienced by anyone, anywhere, and at any time. Sex relegated to the marriage relationship? How backwards and old-fashioned can you get? The stripping of the sacred from sexual intercourse has been one of the key cultural components of a continuously depraved society. We are to become one. Sex does not make us become one. Sex within the parameters of marriage can very much launch us towards the idea of becoming one. How do we know this? Because God told us this would be the case. He wants us to become one. He inspires us to become one. His desire for us is to become one as husband and wife in the marriage context, and sex is a huge part of that reality. If we miss this in any way, shape, or form, we miss what it means to become one. And that is the goal we are fighting for. But there is also another understanding of what it means to become one that is related to, but not the same as, the sexual aspect. And that is to use the idea of becoming one flesh to also... become one.

Enjoining. Remember, we said that God's verbiage regarding becoming one flesh had two manifestations. The first, as we just saw, is the idea of seeing the physical act of sexual intercourse as a part of that process. The second manifestation is the idea of becoming one in a sort of spiritual essence. Think of the idea of sex as becoming one *flesh* and this aspect as the culmination of that idea to ultimately becoming *one*. But this one is a little harder to quantify and define. It's pretty easy to quantify and identify a physical act and its benefits to this overall understanding of our discussion of this paradigm. This idea of becoming one from a spiritual standpoint is a bit more nebulous and eschews conventional quantifiable attempts at describing it. Yet that is exactly what we intend to do.

Let's do it this way. If you remember back to the beginning of this book (seems like a long time ago), I made the observation related to how God decided to describe the relationship between Jesus and His church. And by church, I obviously do not mean a building but people. In fact, in the original language, the word translated as "church" literally means "the called-out ones." And this word is never used in Scripture to describe a building. We, of course, have done a very poor job of relegating that word to mean more a building than the people inside the building. I think many Believers are pretty aware that, even though they use the word "church" to describe a building (nine times out of ten anyway), they also have an awareness that this includes the people inside who actually make up the church. But words mean things. And, too often, we abdicate the main idea about what is meant by the word "church" by using it in a haphazard way. As I stated, in the original language of the New Testament, there was *never* the connotation of the word that leant itself towards a description of a place or a building. It was always to be viewed as the people who make up the church. Nowhere is this more keenly seen than in God's insistence that Jesus' relationship with His church be described as a bridegroom and His relationship with His bride. The level of intimacy evident in that analogy could never be contained within Jesus' relationship with an inanimate object. We see this better in one of the most poignant passages in all of Scripture related to marriage, Jesus, a bride, and a groom.

I mentioned earlier in the book that one of the most misunderstood and misappropriated passages in all of the Bible is found in Ephesians 5:22 which states, "Wives submit to your own husbands as to the Lord." I will not rehash that discussion here, but it is important to note the hermeneutical consequences of errantly fixating on a passage taken completely out of context. For completely incomprehensible reasons, people choose to examine (again, completely out of context) one passage that the world's philosophy has corrupted and condemned while completely ignoring the verses that come after that passage. Amazing, isn't it? Makes you wonder what adversary could be behind the tunnel vision related to this one passage that it would force even Believers not to look any further into His Word. And yet, that is precisely what we must do.

If people can tear themselves away from the misinformed outrage of Ephesians 5:22 long enough, they will see one of the most extraordinary statements made in all of Scripture related to both marriage and the relationship between Jesus and His bride (the church). A few verses later, Paul, under the inspiration of the Holy Spirit, makes an astonishing statement connecting a husband's love for his wife to the love that Christ has for the church. He writes, "Husbands, love your wives, just as Christ loved the church and gave Himself for her" (Ephesians 5:25 NKJV). Paul also includes the reasoning behind this love when he writes that the purpose for this was to "sanctify and cleanse her" and also "to present her to Himself a glorious church...that she should be holy and without blemish" (Ephesians 5:26-27). Now, lest anyone read these words and be confused as to exactly what and who Jesus was referring to in this complex set of statements regarding marriage and our relationship with Him, note that Jesus clearly explains His extended analogy. In Ephesians 5:31, Paul quotes Genesis 2:24 (a passage we have already discussed), which states clearly that a husband and wife are to become one flesh.

Now, we just finished talking about sex within the bounds of marriage being the act that ignites the joining together into one flesh. But also remember, we are investigating this within the context of the summit of the Marriage Pyramid — becoming one. We said that this passage had two complementary meanings in this context. The idea of becoming one *flesh* and the idea of becoming *one*. Here we see the confluence of these two ideas as they relate to the concept of what it means to become one in a marriage. Jesus is using the illustration of human marriage to unravel the mystery of His relationship with His Believers, His children, and His church. In fact, Paul uses the word "mystery" to explain this entire picture with more clarity.

After he quotes Genesis 2:24, Paul writes, "This is a great mystery, but I speak concerning Christ and the church" (Ephesians 5:32 NKJV). Look at what Paul is writing here. Look what God is telling us here. He used a passage (Genesis 2:24) that comes directly from God's mouth as He initiated the very first marriage ceremony and then expanded on the intimacy of that relationship to explain Jesus' relationship with His followers. I know I said this earlier, but it bears repeating. Of all of the examples at His disposal to try and get us to understand the intricacies of His relationship to us, God chose to use the example of marriage to best explain this. What does this say about marriage? He used the ideal relationship between a man and a woman, in the bonds of marriage, as the best illustration of His love and devotion to us. I can't tell you how important it is that we get this and what it says about marriage. Look at the elements listed in Ephesians that reflect this using marriage-type verbiage. These verses, in telling husbands to love their wives, state that they do so by how Christ loved (and loves) the church. Here are the phrases used: "love your wives," "gave Himself for her," "set her apart," "cleanse her," "present her to Himself," "that she should be holy and without blame," "nourishes," "cherishes," "just as the Lord does the church." These are extraordinary words, not just as they relate to God's love for us, but also in reference to how husbands and wives should love and treat and become one with each other.

The culmination of this idea is clearly expressed when Paul brings it full circle as he writes, "For we are members of His body, of His flesh and of His bones" (Ephesians 5:30 NKJV). Just as husband and wife are to become one flesh in their relationship, those who come to faith in Christ also become members of His flesh and His bone. Now you see why Paul used the word "mystery" to explain this reality. All of this follows the phrase "wives submit to your husbands," but we never get this far because we're too busy trying to misinterpret the beginning of the passage. Note that we are to become one flesh with Christ through coming to faith in Him, just as we are to become one flesh with our spouse when we marry them. But, of course, becoming one flesh and one body with Christ is not to be viewed from a physical standpoint, as is suggested in marriage. The one-flesh union with our spouse is manifested in sex; the one-flesh union with Christ is manifested through the Holy Spirit. I know this isn't a book on theology, and I won't belabor this point, but when we came to faith in Christ the Holy Spirit then actually take up residence in our body.

Paul, in his first letter to the Corinthian church, writes, "Or do you not know that your body is the temple of the Holy Spirit who is in you, and you are not your own" (1 Corinthians 6:19 NKJV). In other words, once we are "wed" to Christ by becoming a Believer, there is a clear, spiritual, "becoming one" reality that takes place. God places this reality within the context of the marriage relationship, while using marriage-specific language to explain it. That is how important marriage is. And that is how important becoming one is to a marriage relationship. That's why this idea is the pinnacle of the Marriage Pyramid. While I may have, over the years, tinkered with the idea of switching around the two lowest levels of the Pyramid, I have never, not from day one, flinched from keeping the idea of becoming one as the goal of the Godly marriage. Just as the act of sexual intercourse makes it difficult to tell where one spouse's body ends and the other spouse's body begins, so too does the spiritual connection make it difficult to differentiate one spouse from the other (in the eyes of the spouses themselves).

Once, when I was in the middle of a deployment, Kimberly was talking to a friend about the toll it takes on a family and a marriage. She was trying to find the right example to use, so that the person with whom she was speaking could have some sort of idea as to what prolonged separation from her husband was like. She settled for this: "When he's away like this, I feel as if part of me has been amputated." When I heard this, I knew immediately and spiritually what she meant. We had become one. And when one part of the body is gone, you feel it. It's not the same. It's not pleasant. Oh, you work around it and make due. But the loss is always there, because the loss is a part of you. See what I mean?

That's how important this aspect is. And you will not become one if you don't bond/grow. You will not bond/grow with someone you don't feel safe with. You will not feel safe with someone you do not love in the way that God intended you to love. Therein lies the Marriage Pyramid. Becoming one with my spouse is where my desire is. It's what I want more than anything. But I hope you'll also see that this element of the Pyramid, much like the previous element, does not lend itself to a "list" or "formula" one need simply follow and check off to guarantee oneness. That's why I am taking the approach that I am, in order for you to see the framework of oneness and not the 10-step process to guarantee it. That cannot be done. It simply doesn't work that way. It's also why I am consistently linking it back to a relationship with Christ, in order to reveal its veracity.

Truth is, I cannot become one with my wife apart from becoming one with Christ. It simply cannot happen. Remember, that is the way God designed it. And we cannot have a thing outside of the desire of its Designer. I can take all of the parts of a Harley-Davidson motorcycle and (theoretically) assemble the vehicle. It will not be a Harley-Davidson motorcycle. It will be an imitation of that brand that I created myself. I can ride it. I can enjoy it. But it will never be a Harley-Davidson motorcycle. Likewise, I can never become one with my spouse in the way that God intended apart from God. He designed it. I might be able to come up with an imitation. I might enjoy it. It might even turn out… pretty good. But it will not be oneness. That's why we had to spend this time operationalizing our constructs. If we are going to talk about oneness (and we are), then we have to be working from the same presupposition. Now, you don't have to agree with it, but it is necessary for you to know what I mean when I say "becoming one" and not what you *think* I *might* mean. This pinnacle of the Marriage Pyramid is too important to leave to misinterpretation.

Becoming one is the Everest-like summit of a marriage relationship. I cannot risk being misleading or unclear as we continue this conversation. I fear I may have been both at times, but I leave that to you. For now, let's move on to see if we can get a clearer picture of what becoming one actually looks like.

Isaac and Rebekah.

You know, it's funny. As important as marriage is portrayed throughout the Bible, there really are very few narratives that give us exceptional insight into examples of what an ideal marriage looks like, amongst God's people. We know a great deal about people like Moses, Abraham, Jacob, Joseph, Job, Ruth, Esther, David, Solomon, Isaiah, Peter, and Paul. Many times, we even know a bit about their relationships with their spouses. In fact, with the exception of Joseph and Paul, we know that the rest of the people on the list above were, indeed, married. We even know of some of the exploits between these people and their spouses. We know of Moses' wife's anger at him for not circumcising their son (Exodus 4:24-26), Abraham's deceit in claiming his wife was his sister (Genesis 20:2), Ruth's loving redeemer of a husband (Ruth 3:10-13), Esther's boldness in going before her king/husband (Esther 5:1-4), Job's pain that was only exacerbated by his wife (Job 2:9-10), David's heartache over losing a son born to he and his wife (2 Samuel 12:15-24), Jacob being deceived while trying to marry his wife (Genesis 29:13-28), and Solomon's 700 wives along with 300 concubines (1 Kings 11:3). But we know very little about these marriage relationships in total, from beginning to end. We catch relational snapshots and complicated events that occur during the course of those marriages but, despite the fact that marriage is such an essential part of God's creative acumen, there is scant detail concerning the marital relationships of some of the most important people in God's redemptive history. This is true even though one of the Ten Commandments is directly and specifically related to the marriage relationship (thou shalt not commit adultery). Why is it that this institution seems to have few representative examples in the Bible? I'm not sure. What I am sure about is that there is one huge exception to this reality. Despite the fact that most married couples in the Bible have very little detail about their actual marriage, there is one couple for whom this is not the case. Who is this couple? Isaac and Rebekah.

Okay, I have to be careful to restrain myself here a bit. Primarily (but not exclusively), I am a teacher of God's Word. That is what He has called me to do. It is what He has gifted me to do. It was what I was born to do. I have been preaching/teaching God's Word for more than a quarter of a century in a variety of circumstances. From behind the pulpit of a traditional church, to the middle of the Afghan desert, and everywhere in between. Like most communicators of God's Word, I can easily become a bit long-winded in my exposition of the Bible. It is sort of the nature of the beast. I promise I will fight the urge to do that here. This is a book on marriage, not an exegetical examination of the Old Testament passages related to Isaac and Rebekah. There is so much truth embedded in these passages that it would be very easy (and very desirable to me) to devote a multitude of pages revealing every nugget of truth waiting to be mined from these verses. But that is another book. However, in order for us to see how the Marriage Pyramid looks in real life and what a Godly marriage between two fallen, frail children of God (which we all are, by the way) looks like in real life, we have to go to the Source. And the Source has given us a picture of this by offering us a detailed look into the marriage of two of the most interesting people in all of Scripture. So while I will try to refrain from too much formal exposition of the text, it is necessary that we meet these people whom God chose to reveal the details of their married life. He did, you know. He invites us into the marriage of Isaac and Rebekah from the point of meeting until their last days. And they are the only couple we have this kind of access to. Which tells me that He wants us to pay close attention to this aspect of their lives. They are not perfect. They struggle regularly. And God wants us to see all of it. He wants us to see two imperfect children of His as they work to thrive in the first institution He ever created. And it is something to behold. So let's take a look.

Uniqueness. Before we get to the details related to Isaac and Rebekah, especially as it relates to the Marriage Pyramid, we must first pay homage to one of the more interesting facts about this marriage, as juxtaposed with the vast majority of other marriages mentioned in the Old Testament. Though there are a great deal of similarities, there is one obvious difference that, if we miss it, will make it difficult to see what God wants us to see. The difference is this: among the so-called Patriarchs of the Old Testament, Isaac is the only husband who only ever had one wife. It's true. His father, Abraham, had his wife Sarah, a concubine named Hagar, and later (after Sarah died) married Keturah. Moses married Zipporah and then later an unnamed woman from Cush. Esau had at least three wives. Jacob had at least four wives (or two wives and two concubines). David had at least seven wives, and Solomon had 700 wives. It is possible that Joseph had only one wife, but virtually nothing of their relationship is mentioned outside of the names of the children they had. The point is, we are supposed to notice this marriage relationship between Isaac and Rebekah. It is the *only* marriage to which we have a front-row seat from beginning to end. And this uniqueness alone begs further inquiry and examination. Therefore, we will take a look at these two people individually and how they engaged in a Godly marriage.

Isaac. Since we stated earlier that no one can have the marriage God has designed for them outside of a relationship with God, then is stands to reason that we need to examine this aspect of their lives, along with the traits that sprouted from this relationship. Once again, there is quite a bit of material at our disposal to peruse as we attempt to understand what marriage really looks like. In other words, we know quite a bit about Isaac and his relationship with God. He was, in no uncertain terms, a miracle baby for his parents, Abraham and Sarah. Having been unable to conceive her entire life, God allowed Sarah to become pregnant with Isaac when she was over 90 years old and Abraham was over 100 years old (Genesis 17:17). Though Abraham distrusted God before this and had a son with his wife's servant, Hagar, Abraham considered Isaac his one true son. And after God had blessed the elderly couple with the son they had agonizingly longed for, He made a very odd (which is putting it lightly) request of Abraham. In a move designed to examine Abraham's heart, God ordered that Abraham offer Isaac as a sacrifice. Now, if you don't know the whole of the story and you're tempted to view God as some sort of eternally bored celestial ogre, let's let the story play out.

The vast majority of people, both inside the church and out, miss the nuances of this story, which leads to inevitable misunderstandings. God was not tempting Abraham, nor was He playing a cruel trick. He was actually using this event to strengthen, not only Abraham, but also Isaac. Remember, God had already promised to Abraham that His covenant would be perpetuated through Isaac. It would be pretty hard to do this if Isaac were dead. Still, the command to sacrifice Isaac had to have been disconcerting to the man who had waited so patiently for a son. Nevertheless, once given the command to kill his own son, Abraham dutifully gathered the necessary supplies and headed off.

Upon reaching the outskirts of the site, Abraham says something interesting. Determined to go to the site of the sacrifice with his son while leaving the servants behind, Abraham tells the servants that, after they are through worshipping, "we will come back to you" (Genesis 22:5b). Notice the plural use of the pronoun "we". Abraham fully expected God to work in such a way so that Isaac would not be killed. He didn't know *how* God was going to do this, he just had faith it would be so. In fact, it is a New Testament book that gives us some insight into what Abraham was thinking. The writer states that Abraham concluded "that God was able to raise him up, even from the dead" (Hebrews 11:19a NKJV). So we know that, even if God had asked Abraham to carry out the sacrifice, Abraham knew God could raise him from the dead. But this story is not just about Abraham — it's also about Isaac.

How many of you have either seen an illustration of this scene or a portrayal of it in a book or movie? If you go to YouTube and search for video portrayals of this famous event, you will see a very common element. In virtually every portrayal, you will see that Isaac is imagined as a very young boy. That is almost certainly *not* an accurate portrayal. Even though there are not specific dates and times listed in the Biblical record, most historians and theologians believe that Isaac was, more than likely, over 20 years old. Some Jewish scholars believe he may have been as old as his mid-thirties. Since we know that Abraham was more than 100 years old when Isaac was born, we also know that he was a very, very old man at this point. There is some internal evidence that Isaac was not a small child within the text. The author of Genesis writes, "So Abraham took the wood of the burnt offering and laid it on Isaac his son" (Genesis 22:6a). This statement almost certainly substantiates the claim that Isaac was much older than a young child. Remember, the wood was to be set aflame as a way to burn the sacrifice. Even if Isaac had been a small child, it would have taken a large amount of wood to construct a sacrificial altar that could both hold the child and feed a fire big enough to accomplish the task. A small child would not have been able to carry that much wood. The bottom line is that, at the least, it shows that Isaac was stronger than Abraham. Why is this important?

Because it reveals Isaac's trust in his father and his faith in God. And it is especially this faith in God that is an essential ingredient for a Godly marriage. Look at it this way. Knowing that we now are certain that Isaac was stronger than his 100+ year old father, if he had resisted being placed on the sacrificial altar, would Abraham have been able to physically force Isaac to do so? No, of course not. If Isaac were in his late teens or twenties, he would have easily physically overcome his father and run from this horrific scene. No, instead he was a ready and willing participant in this endeavor because he trusted his father and had faith in his God. Before Abraham even built the altar, Isaac asked his father, "Look, the fire and the wood, but where is the lamb for a burnt offering" (Genesis 22:7b NKJV). We cannot overlook his father's response: "My son, God will provide" (Genesis 22:8a). It was only after this that Abraham placed him on the altar and that Isaac went willingly. This cannot be overstated. Isaac's devotion to his God was a key component of his life. His trust in his father was also almost exclusively due to Abraham's faith in God. No matter how you cut it, faith is the key component in virtually every single interpersonal relationship we are capable of having. And this includes marriage. Which is why we needed to see how this component of Isaac's life influenced his marital relationship with Rebekah. You simply cannot understand one without understanding the other. We will see this more clearly in the section following our examination of Rebekah to see what role (if any) faith played in the development of her character and her willingness to accept an arranged marriage. So let's take a few minutes to get to know Rebekah a little better.

Rebekah. Once again, we do not have to assume a great deal about who Rebekah was and how she developed the marital relationship she had with Isaac. While we obviously do not know every single aspect of their lives together as husband and wife, we do know more about them as a married couple than we know about any other married couple in all of Scripture. As I said before, there has to be a reason for that. There must be a reason why God spilt as much ink (figuratively speaking) as He did allowing us the opportunity to see into the lives of this fascinating couple. The reason will, I hope, become even clearer the more we get to know the two of them. We have just been introduced to Isaac — now we'll meet Rebekah.

Rebekah's story begins in Genesis 24 and concludes with the death of her beloved Isaac, recorded in Genesis 49. But to be able to see what we need to see regarding this picture of Godly marriage, we must acknowledge not only the person Rebekah was, but also the unusual (for our culture) circumstances regarding their marriage in the first place. We see Rebekah's character is intertwined with the total of that story. And it begins with a task assigned to a servant of Abraham (presumably Eliezer, mentioned in Genesis 15:2). The task? Abraham charged his servant to travel back to the land of Abraham's people in order to find a bride for Isaac. Abraham made the servant swear "that you will not take a wife for my son from the daughters of the Canaanites, among whom I dwell" (Genesis 24:3b NKJV). Without getting bogged down in early Jewish Biblical history, remember that God called Abraham away from his home to go to a land that God had provided for His people. The problem was that the land in which Abraham was called was already full of people who worshipped false gods and practiced a false religion. This point is key to understanding why Abraham made this request. It would be easy, with 21st century eyes, to read something into this request that does not exist. Today, if a person were to suggest that a certain ethnic group should only marry members of the same ethnic group and not intermarry with others, that person would be viewed (for the most part) as a racist or bigot. Racism and bigotry played no role whatsoever in this request by Abraham that Isaac marry "his own kind," as opposed to any Canaanite woman. Abraham wasn't concerned about ethnicity, he was concerned about religion.

One of the basic rules of hermeneutics is not to read an ancient document through 21st century eyes. In order to understand what God meant in certain circumstances, we have to be able to understand what it meant to the people at the time, as well as what general lesson He wants us to take away from it some several millennia later. These passages are not *just* for the people of the time, nor are they *just* for us today. They are for both. And while the general theme is universally adaptable, the specific circumstances lend a great deal of understanding from the specific time in which they occur. Not understanding this exegetical reality has led people for generations to conclude that God hates women, endorses slavery, thrives on war, and espouses bigotry. None of this is true if we understand the basic principle that God is trying to reveal while using the cultural conditions on the ground to communicate that principle. Make any sense? Maybe it will when we look at this more closely.

Abraham makes it completely clear that he does not want his son to take a bride from among the Canaanites, whose culture they lived in at the time. There is a reason he fears this. In the book of Ruth, a Jewish family flees to a pagan area to avoid a devastating famine. They remained there for 10 years and, while there, their two sons took brides from among the Edomites. It would stand to reason then that Isaac, upon reaching marrying age, would seek a bride from among the only women he was around: the Canaanites. But Abraham wasn't worried about Isaac marrying a Canaanite, per se. He was very worried that Isaac, marrying a Canaanite, might be corrupted by their religion and abandon faith in the true God. He feared the corrupting influence of the Canaanite religion, not necessarily the Canaanites themselves. Abraham knew that "his people" shared his God and, more importantly, would provide a wife who shared his and Isaac's God. By the way, Abraham's fear was not without merit. In the book of Exodus, when God renews His covenant with the Hebrews, He specifically warns them not to intermarry with people outside of their own. Again, this is not a racist or bigoted command but a faith-driven demand. God gives them the reason why when He states, "lest you make a covenant with the inhabitants of the land... and make sacrifice to their gods... and you take his daughters for your sons... and make your sons play the harlot with their gods" (Exodus 34:15-16 NKJV). God was telling them very clearly that marrying someone with a differing faith will more than likely lead to disaster in the marriage and lead the Believer to abandon his/her faith. In other words, God has to be the centerpiece in any marital relationship. And, of course, God was completely right.

In 1 Kings, we see a clear, documented case of this being exactly correct. The writer makes it clear that, not only does Solomon marry, but he marries 700 women from pagan backgrounds and adds another 300 concubines from pagan backgrounds. The writer then tells us exactly what happened as a result when he writes, "...and his wives led him astray" (1 Kings 11:3b NKJV). This then led the author to also note, "So Solomon did evil in the eyes of the Lord, he did not follow the Lord completely, as David his father had done" (1 Kings 11:6 NKJV). To put this last phrase into perspective, Solomon was a man God had previously bragged about, and his father David had murdered a man to keep his adultery a secret. That's how far a godless marriage had led Solomon away from God. We cannot overstate the importance of a God-filled faith in marriage, especially as it is played out in the lives of Isaac and Rebekah. Remember, we are looking at what elements contributed to Isaac and Rebekah's marriage and also to understand why God saw fit to use these two to give us a glimpse of what it means to become one. Rebekah, at this time in her life, was probably only about 15-18 years old. And she was about to meet a stranger who was going to tell her that a man she had never met sent him, another man she had never met, to bring her to marry yet another man she had never met. An incredible story with some incredible lessons.

We won't go into too many details about the original meeting between Rebekah and the servant at the well, but I encourage you to read the narrative yourself in Genesis 24:1-67. Suffice it to say that the servant, having reached Nahor (a town named after Abraham's brother), initiates his quest with a *very* specific prayer. In a nutshell, he prayed that whatever young woman he spoke to would give him some water. But he didn't stop there. He continued with his prayer, asking that if this be the girl God had chosen, she would then answer him in the affirmative and also volunteer to water his camels as well. He had not even finished his prayer when Rebekah arrived at the well. No sooner did the servant ask for the water than Rebekah offered to water his camels as well. Clearly, this happened only in such a way that God had His hands directly involved. Isaac and Rebekah were clearly meant to be married. God had ordained them to become one, and that was the only way they could have become one. But remember, Rebekah was just a kid. Imagine what she must have been thinking when, after the camels were done, this strange man took a golden nose ring and two gold bracelets, presented them to Rebekah, and asked to go to her house. Because that was exactly what happened.

Remember too that the servant not only knew that God had brought Rebekah to him in his search for Isaac's wife but that he would soon discover that she came from a family that was, in fact, a distant relation to Abraham. Not only did God confirm His intervention into this marriage by answering the servant's prayer, but He also doubled down on the confirmation by leading him to Abraham's family. But notice Rebekah's kindness to this complete stranger through this process. She gave him water and then offered to water his camels. The etiquette of the day was to offer water to a thirsty stranger, but this etiquette did not extend to the accompanying animals. She had an extraordinary kindness that was a part of who she was. And we are not to miss this. She had to have been overwhelmed with the very expensive gifts the stranger lavished on her and also confused by the request to accompany her to her home. But she obviously sensed something special was happening here and so did what she was asked. Yet to suspect she knew exactly what was going on would be a bit of a stretch. It wasn't long after arriving though that the servant began to regale Rebekah and her family with the tale of how he had come to Nahor because of Abraham (whom they all knew, of course) and to find his only son a wife. He then told them of his prayer and how quickly God had specifically answered it and led him directly to Rebekah. He also made sure they understood the role that God played in this entire scenario when he stated, "And I bowed my head and worshiped the Lord, and blessed the Lord God of my master Abraham" (Genesis 24:48a NKJV). This is of the utmost importance to remember. The servant was adamant that this impending marriage was not a result of a desire of a caring father or the luck of finding the "right one." This marriage was a divine appointment with two people of like faith coming together, as designed by the Grand Designer of marriage, for the purpose of having the optimal marriage that is possible. And that is only possible because of the Designer in the first place. That is the entire reason behind this story.

If all we walk away from this passage with is the warm and fuzzy that accompanies a "neat story," we are missing the entire point. This is marriage. The first of God's institutions. It can only be fulfilled if we embrace it in that context. The only way we can become one is by having a relationship with God. The only way we can have the optimal marriage is to adhere to the Designer's plan. That is, in part, what the servant was trying to tell the family and us. And please note the response of the family. After hearing this amazing story, it's not like they were exactly providing a ringing endorsement of this entire plan. Look at the verbiage. After the servant pleads for their cooperation with this betrothal, Laban (Rebekah's brother and Abraham's great-nephew) makes an interesting statement when he says, "This thing comes from the Lord; we cannot speak to you either bad or good" (Genesis 24:50 NKJV). Again, not a ringing endorsement. They were certainly hesitant to let Rebekah go, but they did so because "the Lord has spoken" (Genesis 24:51c NKJV). Even though, personally, they had some trepidation about letting their (more than likely) teenage family member leave with a total stranger, they recognized that God's plan was better than theirs, and they recognized His hand in this entire matter. But what about Rebekah, you may ask.

Well, after having a night to sleep on it, the family began to let their trepidation move into the region of disobedience. As the servant arrived to take Rebekah, the family implored him to let her stay with them a bit longer, assuring him that, after about ten days, they would send her along. Give credit to two people here. First, the servant reminded them that God had ordained this and they dare not delay His will. He continuously made it clear that God, and God alone, was responsible for all of this. If their faith led them all to that conclusion, then delay would simply stoke the fires of doubt. Second, we must give the lion's share of the accolades to Rebekah herself. After the family brings Rebekah out to ask her if she wants to travel over 400 miles with a stranger to marry another stranger (probably thinking she would choose to stay home), Rebekah states simply, "I will go" (Genesis 24:58b NKJV). Three simple words that carry a bucket-load of faith and trust, well beyond the capacity of her years. Why was she able to be so resolute?

Because she had faith that God was at the center of her impending marriage. There is no other logical interpretation. She was a part of a divine plan to ensure her marriage to the man that God had for her, even though she had never met him and couldn't pick him out of a lineup. Faith was the key component, both for Isaac and Rebekah, as they had to come to grips with the reality that they were marrying a person that was a stranger to them. God is the only One Who could pull something like this off. Our culture today could never understand the spiritual implications of God moving like this. In fact, if you've ever seen Hollywood's portrayals of people in arranged marriages, nine times out of ten the story revolves around both parties trying their best to stop the nuptials because they loved someone else. But these portrayals are to miss the point entirely. This story of Isaac and Rebekah is not about the morals or logic of arranged marriages; it is about God being the center of marriage as He designed it. The message isn't that everyone needs to go out and engage in an arranged marriage. He is saying that, when He is involved in the marriage, even an arranged marriage can be the optimal marriage. Please see this. God is the architect of marriage, and He brings people marriage for His purposes and to give us the best shot at marriage we can possibly have. Marriage is not really marriage outside of a relationship with Him. If you ignore the Designer, the design will fail. Either that or it will never be what it was designed to be.

God's presence in this marriage encouraged a young girl to leave her family and home. She somehow found the strength to do this. Not because of her dedication to Isaac — she didn't even know him. Not because of her dedication to her family — they wanted her to stay. Not because of her dedication to the servant — he was a stranger. She engaged in this marriage because God had ordained it. And she knew that if God had ordained it, He would sustain it.

And just take a look at the immediate results. As the caravan containing Rebekah drew closer to Isaac's home, I'm sure nerves were a little on edge. In fact, Isaac went out to the field in the evening alone to meditate (Genesis 24:63). He saw the caravan and began to walk towards it, at which point Rebekah saw him advancing (though she did not know it was he). After discovering it was Isaac, she immediately covered her face (a custom in the ancient Near East to show discretion before one's betrothed) and began the process of getting to know her husband. The husband God had chosen for her. And they began the process of becoming one. In one of the most amazing examples of what I was referring to earlier in this chapter, concerning the two aspects of becoming one, we see that happen after their marriage. The writer of Genesis states that "Isaac brought her into his mother Sarah's tent; and he took Rebekah and she became his wife, and he loved her" (Genesis 24:67 NKJV). Note the verbiage here. When the author states that Isaac "took" Rebekah, he is clearly referencing to sexual intercourse. The first aspect of becoming one flesh.

The author then states, "So Isaac was comforted after his mother's death" (Genesis 24:67c NKJV). Let that sink in for a moment. Sarah, Isaac's mother, had died sometime before he married Rebekah. In fact, Abraham had remarried afterwards, so it had probably been a while since the death took place. Isaac obviously loved his mother and was still mourning her death. That is clear from the text. And who comforted him? Rebekah. The distant relative. The virtual stranger. The person he had never met and been required to marry. That, my friend, is becoming one. That is bonding. That is feeling safe. That is love. And that is what marriage is all about. That is what God wants for each and every one of us. You cannot divorce Isaac and Rebekah's relationship with God from their relationship with each other. You cannot do that with marriage at all. Let's wrap this section up by doing something kind of fun. Let's take a look, briefly, at the totality of Isaac and Rebekah's marriage and relate it to the elements in the Marriage Pyramid. Is there a correlation to the ideas I have put forth in this book with marriage relationships in the real world, with real people? And make no mistake, Isaac and Rebekah were real people in the real world. They were not perfect. You will see this as we examine their marriage, their quest to become one, through the lens of the Marriage Pyramid. You will see their successes and their failures. And you will see their reliance on God as the centerpiece of that marriage. So let's take each of the four levels of the Pyramid and examine their marriage and how it applies.

Love. As was stated in the section of the book dealing with this construct, love is the foundational element of every marriage. However, if you also remember, in order to completely grasp what exactly this word means within the context of marriage, we have to rely, not on the culture's understanding of love, but on God's. We do not need to rehash the entire section here, but we do need to be reminded that love is not, in and of itself, an emotion. It certainly has feelings associated with it, but love, as it is expressed in Scripture, is more a decision than a reaction. Because if we can *fall* into love, it stands to reason that we can *fall* out of love. It may be helpful here for you to go back to Chapter two and reacquaint yourself with this conversation. It is of the utmost importance that we get our understanding of what love means from a Biblical standpoint, in order then to be able to see its necessity in a marriage relationship. I *choose* to love my wife regardless of her actions. She *chooses* to love me, faults and all. It is this understanding of love from the Essence of love (God) that enables Jesus to be able to tell us to love our enemies (Matthew 5:43-47). Jesus is certainly *not* saying that we should have good, happy, tranquil feelings about our enemies because that is not the measuring stick for love. If we view love as a concerted effort and decision on our part, it makes it much easier to love our enemies. How does this play out in the lives of Isaac and Rebekah?

Simply put, theirs was an arranged marriage. Abraham's servant was dispatched more than 400 miles away to find Isaac a bride. I cannot, for a moment, believe that Isaac was not aware of this quest. He embraced the arranged marriage without any of the "normal" accoutrements related to courtship and "falling" in love. He loved and trusted his father. He loved and trusted God. Therefore, he would love the wife God had chosen for him. It is key to understand this caveat. Isaac would not have viewed his wife as having been chosen by Abraham or by Abraham's servant. He would have viewed his wife as having been chosen by God Himself. And if God had chosen his bride for him, then Isaac would have no problem choosing to love the wife selected for him, even though he had no idea what she was like. He didn't have to "fall" in love; he chose to love. The final verse in Genesis 24 contains these amazing words: "And he took Rebekah and she became his wife, and he loved her" (Exodus 24:67b NKJV). Think about this for a moment. Isaac had not even met Rebekah prior to this. Though we don't know exactly how long the betrothal lasted, the text seems to suggest a very quick turnaround from the time he first saw his veiled fiancé until the time they were wed. And he *loved* her. This was no emotion-based, Hollywood-designed portrayal of love rooted almost exclusively in how the two of them "felt" about each other. This was a love designed by God for the most sacred institution of marriage. Were feelings associated with this love? Of course. "So Isaac was comforted after the death of his mother" (Genesis 24:67c NKJV). It felt good for Isaac to be Rebekah's husband. However, the feelings were not the arbiter of the veracity of the love. He didn't know he loved her because of the feelings. He had the feelings because he knew that he loved her. There is an ocean of difference between those two ideas. He loved God. God chose Rebekah for him. Therefore, he loved Rebekah with the love that could have only originated from God. That is precisely how it is supposed to work.

What about Rebekah? She obviously loved her family. They obviously knew that this entire event was orchestrated, ordained, and blessed by God (Genesis 24:51). Therefore, so did Rebekah. She was even given an "out" by her family, who wanted her to stay home for another 10 days. She did not take it. Why? There is only one logical explanation. She knew that God was the architect of all of this in order to ensure that she would marry a man she may have had no idea even existed up to that point. She agreed with the spiritual assessment of a complete stranger (Genesis 24:56) rather than acquiesce to the emotions-based plea of her own flesh and blood (Genesis 24:55-58). There was absolutely no way she could have agreed to any of this if it had been based on the emotions of love. In fact, it would be absurd to suggest she had *any* emotional feelings towards Isaac at this point in her life. And yet, she committed to be his wife. Why? Because she knew that God would provide the love necessary for a marriage like this not only to survive but thrive. She didn't need the feelings we so often confuse with love itself because she had already chosen to love her future husband, by and through the power of God.

I can't tell you how important it is to see this. If the base level of the Marriage Pyramid is correct (and it is), we actually see it in action here in the life of Isaac and Rebekah. Before they ever laid eyes on each other, heard each other's voice, knew the color of each other's eyes, heard each other's laugh, hurt at each other's tears, they loved each other. And they did so because they had tapped into the Source of all love. Extraordinary, isn't it? That is the only reasonable explanation for their love. They certainly didn't "fall" in love. Nor did they experience the amazing feelings associated with meeting and getting to know each other. They simply chose to love each other before meeting because God had ordained their marriage. As He ordains all of them that adhere to His design. And because the feelings didn't *cause* them to fall in love, then an ebbing of those feelings would not lead them to abandon that same love. We see here the Marriage Pyramid in action with real people. Because of the accurate understanding of love, Isaac and Rebekah would later be able to withstand incidents that did, in fact, place tremendous pressure on other aspects of the Pyramid. We will see, as we continue, that theirs was not a perfect marriage and was, at times, fraught with difficulties. But because the foundation was sound, they never lost this aspect of their marriage as they travailed up and down the rest of the Pyramid throughout their lives (which happens to *all* marriages). I hope you see how they appropriated the first level of the Pyramid and how it maintained them throughout the rest of their lives. But let's move on.

Safety. If you remember, when we discussed this aspect of the Pyramid back in Chapter three, we made a point to distinguish between physical safety and emotional safety. I made the point that we are all pretty savvy to the fact that physical and emotional abuse will cause tremendous difficulty in a marriage and will keep every couple from advancing up the Pyramid. In fact, it is so obvious that I paid little more than lip service to this idea because it so universally accepted and understood. I was, of course, not dismissing its importance and impact. I was simply trying to state that, at this point in our culture, I should not have to convince you that the Big Three (physical abuse, substance abuse, and adultery) are really, really bad for your marriage. For our purposes, we needed to focus on an aspect of safety that is way under the radar but is responsible for so many couples not having the optimal marriage. That is why I focused on this idea of emotional safety and how drastically important is to the marriage relationship. As before, we have already discussed this in detail in Chapter three. If you feel the need to go back and re-read this section before we see it in the lives of Isaac and Rebekah, please do so. It is important that we have the philosophical foundations of these constructs in place if we are to understand them when we see them in the lives of this amazing couple.

Much of their safety, as with their love, was solely rooted in God. Even from the beginning, we see two examples (one from each person) of how emotionally safe they must have felt and how that safety was related to God and His provision. Let's start with Rebekah and, once again, go back to her time with her family. It is often a temptation with Bible readers to scan the text and miss a significant learning moment. We have a tendency to do this most often with very short verses or verses that just seem to be there to move the narrative along. One of the most obvious examples of this is the shortest verse in the entire Bible, John 11:35: "Jesus wept." Two simple words that we have a tendency to want to zip right past to get to the "main" emphasis of the story or event. In doing so, however, we miss more than would be thought possible. There are multiple lessons and sermons that could be (and I'm sure have been) preached on those two simple but powerful words. Such is the case with the narrative under discussion here. We have mentioned this passage a few times, but I would not want anyone to miss the more subtle insights as it relates to a lot of things but to the Pyramid in particular. The verse is Genesis 24:57b: "And she said, 'I will go.'" That was the answer this (probable) teenager gave when given the chance to either go with a total stranger to a strange land and marry a total stranger, or stay with her family. Let me ask you: where do you think Rebekah would have *felt* safer? Is there anyone reading this that would actually try to suggest that she would have felt safer with this stranger, traveling more than 400 miles to marry a different stranger, than she would have felt with her own family in her own home? Of course not.

Home, family, familiar surroundings — these are the hallmarks of what it means to feel safe. Strangers, moving, uncertainty — these are the hallmarks of what it means to *not* feel safe. In other words, there is no reason why Rebekah should have felt safe enough to make the decision she did and put herself in an extremely vulnerable position. Only her unwavering faith in God could have begun the almost supernatural process of loving and feeling safe with a husband she had not met and a family she did not know. This is both from a physical *and* emotional standpoint. Remember, when we choose to love someone, we become intimately vulnerable to that person. If you recall from our earlier conversation, this creates a very complex relationship. My wife can hurt me more than any other person on the planet. Which means she is (potentially) the most dangerous person to me on the planet. This serves as the crux of the entire idea of emotional safety. We will never move beyond the second level of the Pyramid if we do not feel emotionally safe with the person who is, potentially, the most dangerous person in the world to us. The potential for my wife to hurt me is there. I just trust that she will not reach that potential. I must feel emotionally safe with my wife, or I will keep her at arm's length emotionally. If I don't feel safe, or if that safety is threatened, it is human nature for me to scramble to safety. At my wife's expense, if need be. Yet here is Rebekah, already well on her way to embracing that level of safety before she even met her husband. This just goes to show how important this aspect of the Pyramid is.

And what of Isaac? He too shows a remarkable level of trust in his new bride after they are married. Notice again the reality that Isaac "was comforted after his mother's death" (Genesis 24:67c). If nothing else, this passage illustrates that, at a very early stage in their marriage, Isaac accepted a significant level of vulnerability towards his wife. He shared with her his feelings of loss at the death of his mother and entrusted one of his most intimate moments with a wife he, technically, barely knew. He could have only done so because he felt safe with her. He could have only felt that safe, that quickly, because of the Godly love they had for each other. I hope you're seeing here how the Pyramid works and what it looks like in real life. But you may be saying, "Yeah, but they're in the Bible, and this all sounds like a fairy-tale, too-good-to-be-true story." Nothing could be further from the truth.

Because, as we have seen the positive reactions to an emotionally safe environment between husband and wife in the life of Isaac and Rebekah, we also are privy to what happens when that safety is shattered. Later in their life, Isaac and Rebekah had to leave their home due to a famine to seek refuge in a land under a pagan king (Genesis 26:1). Isaac must have been afraid because God took this time to reassure him that He had made a covenant with Isaac and that all would be well, even in the midst of a powerful, pagan king (Genesis 26:1-5). However, fear is the mortal enemy of safety. When the men who lived in that land began to inquire about Rebekah, Isaac lied to them and claimed she was his sister (as his father, Abraham, had done with Sarah some time back). His justification for the lie was that he surmised that if the men saw how beautiful Rebekah was and that she was his wife, they would kill him and take her. Now, I don't know if that was a rational fear based on the culture of these people, but it was certainly unfounded based on the reassurance God had just given him. Nevertheless, he was afraid. So let's look at it this way. Isaac was in fear for himself and his safety, so he told a lie that then put at risk Rebekah and *her* safety. If Rebekah was simply Isaac's sister, then she would be in the position for men to come and seek after her for a relationship. Isaac saved himself by endangering his wife, along with the reality that Rebekah had to constantly hear Isaac claim she was not his wife.

Let me ask you, how safe do you think Rebekah felt with Isaac after that? Remember, the marriage relationship is the most intimate and sacred of any relationship we could possibly have, and that includes our relationship with our children. God said, "Therefore a man shall leave his father and mother and be joined to his wife, and they shall become one flesh" (Genesis 2:24 NKJV). We do not become one with our parents or our kids; we become one with our spouse. If we miss this, we miss a lot. So here was Isaac, the love of her life, her "one," with whom she had the most intimate relationship she could have with anyone, telling people she wasn't even his wife. And he did so to protect *himself*, not her. If, prior to this event, Isaac and Rebekah had been existing as husband and wife at the top of the Pyramid, then the moment he uttered those words and came up with that plan they plummeted to the very bottom of it. There is no way she could have felt emotionally safe with a husband who would place her physical safety and her emotional safety behind his perceived physical safety. See what I mean? This is the Pyramid at work. They can't experience "being one" if they don't bond/grow. They are not going to "bond/grow" with someone they do not feel safe with. There is no "safety" if there is no love. I hope you're catching this. This model is always fluid. Our choices and, sometimes, our circumstances will dictate where we are on the Pyramid at any given time. And that doesn't mean that there haven't been acts prior to this that met all of the criteria of an optimal marriage.

This example is a perfect picture of that. It is more about what level of the Pyramid you are experiencing at this time than if you have ever been there. For example, let's say you have a married couple, and both happen to be committed Believers. They have been married for more than 20 years and, like all marriages, have experienced some issues along the way. But by and large, they have been at or near the top of the Pyramid for the majority of their marriage. They understand Godly love, work to provide emotional safety, love being and growing with each other, and have a pretty good understanding of what it means both to become one flesh and to become one. Let's say the husband goes out of town for a week and, during that time, has a massive failure. Something he has never done before or has not even been tempted to do before. Overcome with guilt and the desire to confess to his wife, he goes home and does so. Now, the wife is sailing along with the knowledge that she and her husband (at this time in their life) are at the top of the Pyramid. She would gladly and truthfully tell you that she and her husband are experiencing what it means to become one. Then, her husband breaks the news to her. Obviously, at that moment, she no longer is experiencing "oneness" with her husband. In fact, she certainly no longer feels safe with him (he has become the most dangerous person in the world to her) and is not even sure she loves him anymore. The betrayal is just too much (probably why Jesus grants divorce in cases of adultery).

For the sake of argument, let's assume that she still loves him but obviously does not feel safe with him and certainly is not experiencing oneness right now. But that doesn't mean that she has never experienced that. This also doesn't negate the becoming "one flesh" that God mentioned as a part of the act of sexual intercourse. We are talking about the living out of this paradigm.

The experiencing of these various constructs. Not experiencing them does not mean that you are not really married or that you can't even stay married for 40 years. You will just not have the optimal marriage possible. And the optimal marriage possible does NOT mean that you will stay at the top level all of the time. And when you're not at the top level for a while, it doesn't mean that you will not get back there and experience it again. A marriage not at the top of the Pyramid is not a failed marriage, per se. It is an unfulfilled marriage. It is not the optimal marriage. But it does not indicate failure. The whole idea behind writing this at all is to provide some type of framework so that we can experience the best marriage God has for us. "Experience" is the key word here. How much of this type of marriage are we experiencing at the moment? Remember the pain scale we mentioned earlier? Just as we are asked where we are on the pain scale, so we must use the Pyramid to see where we are in that construct. Are we experiencing the best of what we can in our marriage? If not, what has happened to thwart that? Then, what do we do to get back to that spot? That's the entire idea behind the Pyramid. It's not to find our place on the scale and bemoan it (or, consequently, to rest on our laurels) but to see where we are on the scale at the time and to be aware of it and how to improve it. It's just that simple. We will not always be where we want to be. We will fail often at that, and that's okay. That is the price we must pay for the reality that sin corrupts everything it touches. I'm just trying to provide what I think is a Biblically based target to aim at. Because if we aim at nothing, we'll hit it every time. And we do that too often in marriage. That's what this excursion into the life of Isaac and Rebekah is about. They experienced every level of the Pyramid. Sometimes they were up and sometimes down. Such is the nature of being married. I just want us to be encouraged by the fact that they struggled with these constructs and yet still had a Godly marriage. That's the whole reason behind this book and looking at this couple. So, with that being said, let's move on to the next level of the Pyramid and how it played out in the marriage of Isaac and Rebekah.

Oneness. As has been stated time and again in this book, the idea of what it means to be one in the marriage context is often difficult to quantify. Often, the best way to recognize it is to know it when we see it. I hope you are seeing in this paradigm that we should expect that things will happen within our marriage that will affect where we are on the Pyramid. As I've stated, sin is the great corruptor. We are all sinful. Therefore, sin corrupts us and the things we care about most, including marriage. However, that does not keep us from being able to experience what God intended for marriage, including oneness. There will be things that thwart us and discourage us. And if we had to depend on our own strength and our own "goodness" to overcome these things, that would be a problem. But if we are Believers and Christ lives within us, we can experience the best of what God has for us in our marriage. It may be a bit up and down. In fact, it will be up and down. But as the Pyramid shows, we can know where we are and how the innate power of God that resides in us can help us experience what it means to truly be *married*.

That is exactly what we are going to see in the life of Isaac and Rebekah as we examine the pinnacle of the Pyramid — what it looks like in real life, what causes it to wane, and what it means to get it back again. It is amazing that God has given us insight into this incredible marriage and all of the foibles that accompanied it. Part of that is to be able to let us know that it's going to be alright. Even when it seems it won't be. There is forgiveness and reconciliation, even in the midst of severe betrayal. And that we can still know what it is to be "one," even when we feel so far away from each other while in the midst of turmoil. So let's take a look at some examples of what it looked like in the life of Isaac and Rebekah when they both experienced being one and the actions taken to blunt that experience. It is a fascinating story.

Since there is much more about Isaac and Rebekah's marriage that we *don't* know than we *do*, there is also much we might have to speculate about. Again, despite the fact that these people are considered "heroes of the faith," they were regular old folks with a (probably) regular old marriage. We saw earlier that they endured a significant issue when Isaac lied about Rebekah being his wife and, as a result, actually put Rebekah's physical and emotional well-being in danger. However, we also see examples of their desire to experience oneness sprinkled throughout the narrative as well. In one particularly meaningful event, we see both Isaac and Rebekah's desire for a child. We have a tendency to take things like this for granted, but let's take a closer look at this. Nowhere else in the marriage relationship do we see the intersection of becoming one *flesh* and becoming *one* so amazingly illustrated as we do in the desire and consummation of having a child. This reality allows us to actually take part in the creation of life by permission of the God of the universe. Be sure, we do not actually create the life. God alone is responsible for that. However, He does allow us to take part in this process that, not only produces a life, but gives new meaning to what it means to become one. He uses the act that causes us to become one flesh (sexual intercourse) to partake in the creation of a life that actually shares the DNA of each partner. This is a tangible example of how becoming one flesh produces a result that is a remarkable symbol of what becoming one looks like. Please do not misunderstand. Having a child together does not ensure experiencing oneness. Not having a child (or not being able to) does not ensure you will *not* experience oneness with your spouse. This is simply a *picture* of how these things work together and how they look in real life.

Note the verbiage in Genesis when the author writes, "Now Isaac pleaded with the Lord for his wife, because she was barren; and the Lord granted his plea and Rebekah his wife conceived" (Genesis 25:21 NKJV). Did you catch the most precious part of that statement? Isaac didn't just simply cry out to God. It is interesting to note that the author wanted to make sure we understood that he pleaded to God *"for his wife* [italics mine]." He didn't cry out for God to give him a son; he cried out that God would give his wife a child. By this point, it is estimated that Rebekah had probably been barren nearly 20 years. Isaac ached for his wife. She was in pain, and he was experiencing that pain with her. That's what happens when you're experiencing oneness.

I remember the wedding ceremony with my wife as if it were yesterday, rather than nearly 30 years ago. I don't remember all of the words the pastor spoke, but I remember these: "When you experience joy, the joy will be doubled. When you experience pain, the pain will be halved." I think about those words all the time. And I have come to view them as what it means (at least in part) to become one. Isaac felt Rebekah's pain. He prayed because of Rebekah's pain. He pleaded with God because of Rebekah's pain. And, because they were one, he bore part of Rebekah's pain. He felt it. He mourned it. If you are not experiencing what it means to become one, you are not able to do and feel what Isaac felt and did. Later, when their son, Esau, married multiple wives outside of their faith, the author of Genesis tell us, "And they (the pagan wives) were a grief of mind to Isaac and Rebekah" (Genesis 26:35). Imagine the pain they were feeling, especially in light of the faith and trust they had in God when He ordained their marriage to each other as complete strangers. Any parent that has had a traumatic experience with their wayward child knows that this kind of trauma can make or break a marriage. The parents can blame each other, or they can share the burden. Isaac and Rebekah chose to share the burden because they were experiencing the oneness that God intended for them. What a tremendous example God has given us here so that we can understand what it looks like when a couple is experiencing oneness. But there is another side to that coin.

Remember, no marriage is perfect. And no marriage stays at the top of the Pyramid all of the time. The Pyramid is a temperature gauge to the extent that it allows us to see where we are in our marriage and what might be keeping us from getting to where we want to be. That example is fully illustrated in the story of Isaac and Rebekah as we begin to see them slip from that experience of oneness and down the Pyramid in a very dramatic way. More than anything, I want this book to be encouraging rather than discouraging to the reader. I want this to be a tool that is useful to getting us where God wants us to be in our marriage and not to despair when we fall short. That's why I am so encouraged when I see the example of Isaac and Rebekah. When we take a glimpse into their marriage, we see the exultation that accompanies a marriage in lock-step with what God has designed. We also see the heartache that inevitably winds its way into every marriage but that doesn't have to remain. Yes, trouble (even disaster) will, at times, find its way into the relationship we have with our spouse. It will hurt. It will confuse. It will plunge us into a level of the Pyramid where we do not like to be. But we do not have to stay there. We are about to view tragedy and betrayal as it wedges itself into this Godly marriage and, ultimately, how the marriage is able to thrive afterwards. That's the whole idea behind the Pyramid. We may be at a lower level of the construct, but we don't have to remain there. Such was the case with Isaac and Rebekah.

It is interesting to note how this tragedy begins to unfold and how the chink in the armor of oneness actually begins. Let's take a look at a very interesting passage that seems to portend the impending tragedy. The author of Genesis tells us, "And Isaac loved Esau because he ate of his game, but Rebekah loved Jacob" (Genesis 25:28 NKJV). In case you don't know the story, allow me to fill in the blanks a bit. After Rebekah conceived, it did not take long before she realized that, not only was she carrying twins, but that the sibling rivalry that would ensue after birth was actually evident while they were still in the womb (Genesis 25:21-23). When Rebekah asked God why this was happening, the Lord answered her with words that need close scrutiny. God said, "Two nations are in your womb... and the older shall serve the younger" (Genesis 25:23a,d NKJV). That last phrase is the key one. In that culture, the eldest son in the family was the preferred son and the chief heir of his father. All other subsequent sons would receive lesser praise, inheritance, and family stature. Here, God was turning that traditional order upside down (as He was wont to do from time to time). God was clearly saying that it would be the younger son who would receive the inheritance and blessing reserved for the oldest. This becomes key to understanding the issues as they later develop.

The struggle, according to God, would not only take place in the womb but would follow the nations that would spring from each son. Of course, Jacob would be part of the lineage of the Israelites while Esau's family lineage would bring forth the Amalekites, with whom Israel would be in conflict for centuries. Of course, neither Isaac nor Rebekah knew this at the time. They were just rightfully excited about finally having children after being denied for 20 years. However, it is ironic that it would be one of the most important moments of their lives that would lead them to one of the darkest moments of their marriage. The birth of their sons was, if nothing else, very unusual.

Their grappling in the womb continued during the birth process so that when the first son, Esau, emerged, his brother,

Jacob, was so close behind that he literally "took hold of Esau's heel" (Genesis 25: 26a NKJV). See the picture here? The eldest son emerged from the womb with his brother holding fast to his heel while still struggling to be the first one out. And that's not all of the description we have of the boys as they grew into adulthood, as the author of Genesis states, "And Esau was a skillful hunter, and a man of the field; but Jacob was a mild man, dwelling in tents" (Genesis 25:27b NKJV). Again, why this information? Why would God want to include a bit of information that, on the surface, may not seem to add too much to the overall narrative related to these two brothers? It seems a bit out of place. But hermeneutics 101 tells us unequivocally that there is no such thing as an inconsequential bit of information in the Bible. There is a reason why God included this bit of material for us, and I believe much of it has to do with having us understand what can intrude into a marriage that might keep a couple from experiencing oneness. Why might we come to this conclusion? To put it in the vernacular that we might find familiar in our culture today, it seems as if we are being told that Esau was a "daddy's boy" while Jacob was a "momma's boy." These terms, by the way, are not meant to be a pejorative but to present an accurate description and to illustrate the genesis (pardon the pun) of the impending trouble.

Lest you think I may be exercising a bit of a theological reach here, take a look at the following verse once more: "And Isaac loved Esau because he ate of his game, but Rebekah loved Jacob" (Genesis 25:28 NKJV). It is abundantly clear that Isaac had chosen his "favorite" of the two because of Esau's prowess as a hunter and provider, while Rebekah had chosen Jacob because of his desire to remain at home (in the tent), presumably with his mother. I hope you're seeing the seeds of discourse here, not only between the brothers, but also (and more importantly) between a husband and wife. Note especially the use of the word "but" in that passage. Virtually all of the most well-known translations include that word in their verbiage. In this case, the word seems to be used to suggest an underlying difference in the relationship between the parents and their children. Isaac loved Esau, "*but*" Rebekah loved Jacob. This seems to suggest the parents had clearly taken sides in opposition to each other regarding their own children. My bride and I have four children. When we say that we don't have a favorite or that we don't love one more than the other, that is not mere empty rhetoric motivated by cultural mores. It is simply the truth. In fact, I don't think we are capable of loving any of them over and above the others. We admire their differing strengths and lament their differing weaknesses, but we do not value any of them more than the others.

Here, we see two parents that have staked their claim on the same familial land but on opposite sides of a fence. The point is, how can a husband and wife experience oneness when they are on opposing sides of love regarding their very own children? The short answer: they can't. The children were a tangible symbol of their oneness, but they divided their love for their children and, in doing so, divided their oneness. Logically speaking, you can't experience oneness when you are divided. Especially when you are divided over something that is closely related to the idea of your oneness in the first place. The moment they chose drastically opposing sides in this relationship, they erected a barrier to oneness. That's not to say that couples cannot disagree about things. They certainly can and do. And that disagreement (depending on how much skin in the game they have with it) does not necessarily mean that they cannot experience oneness. But the more important the subject of the disagreement, the more of an impediment it will be for becoming one. The opposition here, described in the marriage between Isaac and Rebekah, cannot be overstated. This was a huge stumbling block that, if not corrected, would lead to an inevitable tragedy. And that is exactly what happened. That is, at least in part, why we have this information in the first place. God is trying to show us, some 4,000 years after the fact, what types of things (if left unaddressed) will lead to a lack of oneness. He wants us to see the inevitability of this reality. And He does so by showing us the all too predictable consequence of these actions (or lack thereof).

Remember, God told Rebekah before the children were born that it would be the second-born, Jacob, that would receive the blessing normally reserved for the eldest. We don't want to get too bogged down in Old Testament Jewish traditions, but we must understand some of the nuances if we are to see how this tragedy unfurls and how it affects Isaac and Rebekah's oneness. God did tell Rebekah that Esau would serve Jacob, but we don't know if He told Isaac. And we don't know if Rebekah told Isaac. We should assume either that she did tell him and Isaac didn't believe her or she didn't and, therefore, Isaac had no idea that the lineage of the covenant God made with him would be carried out, not by Esau, but by Jacob. Either way, there were some horrible communication skills on display here. The tradition of that time was that, as the father (the patriarch of the family) was dying or getting close to dying, he would call for the eldest son and pronounce a blessing on that son as a sort of passing of the torch. We see this played out in Genesis as Isaac calls for Esau and bids him to go out and hunt some game and prepare him a tasty meal so that "my soul may bless you before I die" (Genesis 26:4c NKJV). Here is the thing we must remember about that time period. To the Hebrews of that day, a word spoken was a deed done. They believed there was power in words, especially as they related to things of this nature. They did not hand out blessings haphazardly nor did they even conceive of the possibility they could "take it back." Once the patriarchal blessing had been bestowed, there it would stay. In other words, if

Isaac pronounced the blessing on Esau, not only would he receive the monetary and cultural advantages pursuant to the blessing, but he would receive the lineage of the covenant God had made first to Abraham and then to Isaac. However, God had already determined that Jacob would be the recipient of these blessings. So there was a problem.

Now, while Isaac was talking to Esau, Rebekah was listening in. And because they were not experiencing oneness as it relates to the marriage relationship (because of their selfish opposition related to the children), going in and solving this problem with her husband was not an option. They were at odds with each other. That does not usually lead to coming together to solve a problem. Such was the case here. Isaac was communicating with his "favorite" and was preparing to pass on the blessing to him, yet Rebekah was seeing that her "favorite" was about to be passed over for the blessing she wanted for him. See the problem? In a perfect scenario, this would have been a time where the husband and wife might come together in order to solve a difficult problem regarding the children. But remember, they were in conflict with each other regarding the children. Add to the fact the possibility that there were spiritual issues involved here and that just exacerbates the situation. Even though it is possible, it seems highly unlikely that Isaac did *not* know of God's desire to bless Jacob instead of Esau. Though the text does not explicitly state that Isaac was aware of God's plan, it seems unlikely that neither God nor Rebekah told him about this. So let's go under the assumption that Isaac did, in fact, know of the plan but, for whatever reason, decided not to go along with it. It would not be the first time Isaac disobeyed God to do what he wanted to do. His lie maintaining that Rebekah was his sister, rather than his wife, was a clear case of Isaac's lack of trust in God's sovereignty. He was not immune to disobedience to God simply because he was a hero of the faith.

Therefore, if Isaac was aware that he was, in fact, supposed to bless Jacob but simply could not bear to pass over his oldest (and favorite) son, then we can see his failure as the spiritual leader of the home. You can see why the spouses were at odds with each other. And you can see (though not condone) why Rebekah ended up doing what she did.

Upon hearing Isaac's conversation with Esau, Rebekah immediately embarked on a deception of monumental proportions. In short, Rebekah conspired with Jacob to deceive Isaac into blessing Jacob instead of Esau. It was premeditated, sinful, and devastating to all involved. The plan was intricate to say the least. Rebekah told Jacob to get two goats so that she could prepare a meal that she knew Isaac loved. The idea was to get Isaac to think that it was Esau who had prepared the meal from game he had been out hunting. Then Jacob was to take the meal to Isaac (whose eyesight was fading), pretending to be Esau, and take the blessing. Notice I did not say "steal" the blessing. Because what must not be lost in all of this was that, prior to this event, Esau actually traded his birthright to Jacob for a bowl of stew (Genesis 25:29-34). Yeah, I know. He must have been pretty hungry to pay such a large price for a bowl of soup. It must have been really, really good soup. Remember, to the Hebrews of this day, a word spoken was a deed done. When Esau traded his birthright to Jacob, Jacob literally became the eldest son, with all of the advantages of that position. Notice, Esau did *not* seem interested in letting Isaac know about this chain of events. Once Isaac made the declaration that he would bless Esau as the first-born, Esau did not tell Isaac that it was, in fact, Jacob who was now the first-born. Must have slipped his mind. I hope you see the dysfunction present here with enough blame to go around for everyone.

So when Jacob was given this plan by his mother, he did not complain about the deception as much as he worried that he might get caught. He even made this clear to his mother when he said, "Esau my brother is a hairy man, and I am a smooth-skinned man. Perhaps my father will feel me and I shall seem to be a deceiver to him" (Genesis 27:11-12 NKJV). He was worried about being caught way more than he was about the plan as a whole. Therefore, his mother told him to put goat skins on his body to fool Isaac into believing it was Esau. It worked. Even though Isaac was suspicious about Jacob's voice, he felt the goat skins, proclaimed him to be Esau, and passed the blessing onto his second-born son. Despite the fact that this was exactly what God wanted to happen, He did not want anyone to engage in lying and deceit to accomplish His will. In fact, when we take God's matters into our hands, it always ends up in disaster. The fact that Jacob was blessed surely shows God's sovereign will can never be thwarted by our heartiest efforts, but the manner in which it took place showed the devastation that is wreaked upon those who engage in deception to harm their own family. Though God's will was done, the sin involved in all of this had terrible consequences.

Once the deception was discovered, Jacob had to flee his home and live with relatives. He never saw his mother again. Esau sought to kill him. He had an uncle that took advantage of him for 14 years. Conflict and exile were a part of his family life from that day forward. And there is an interesting remark made by Rebekah when Jacob told her he worried about what his father might think of him because of this heinous plan. He worried that instead of blessing, if his ruse was discovered, he would receive a curse from his father. Rebekah stated, "Let your curse be on me, my son" (Genesis 27:13a NKJV). Think about that for a moment. Here is a wife who was in such a bad place with her husband that she was willing to receive a curse from him because of her actions. Do you think she was feeling oneness with Isaac at that time? Do you think she was experiencing growth or bonding at that time? Do you think she was feeling safe with him? She expected him to curse her — I'm not sure exactly what that meant in that context, but it doesn't sound good. The best that marriage could hope for at that moment was love. And not love because they were *feeling* it. My guess is that, during this time, love was the *last* thing they were actually *feeling*. I am sure they were feeling anger, frustration, betrayal, disappointment, hopelessness, and any other negative reaction you can name. But because their love was not *based* on those feelings, there would be hope that they could navigate through this horrendous difficulty they found themselves in. Before we leave this story though, let's see what happens at the end. And I mean the very end. The next to last chapter in Genesis gives us the narrative of Jacob's death. Having fathered sons that would become the 12 Tribes of Israel, Jacob's life came to an end. The author of Genesis tells us that he was buried in a cave near a field called Machpelah. In fact, though he was in Egypt at the time, he longed to be buried in the family plot (so to speak) with one of his wives, Leah. Jacob said, "There they buried Abraham and Sarah his wife, there they buried Isaac and Rebekah his wife" (Genesis 49:31 NKJV). After all that they had been through, despite the difficulties in their life together, Isaac never took another bride, either while he was married to Rebekah or afterwards. And when he died, as he had done in life, he was by her side. It wasn't always easy. It wasn't always fun. But theirs was a marriage rooted in God's design for that most sacred of institutions. They experienced oneness and then watched it wane. They hung on when all they had was love and watched as that grew into oneness.

Concluding thoughts.

I know we've spent some time looking at the married life of Isaac and Rebekah. And I hope that you have seen that the juice was certainly worth the squeeze. What a remarkable couple and what a wealth of information we have about these two. The fact that God would allow us to have such insight into the marriage between these two amazing (but flawed) people is jaw-dropping. Think about this. Here are the things we know about Isaac and Rebekah that can be said about no other married couple in the entire Bible. We know who they are before they are ever married. We know who they are before they are ever betrothed. We know of both of their families before they were married. We know where they lived before they were married. We know the plan to bring them together. We know how the plan was carried out. We know the first time they met. We know their desperation regarding their childlessness. We know their love for each other. We know they trusted God in their marriage. We know their shortcomings. We know their lies. We know their deceptions. We know that neither of them ever married anyone else. We know they, to this day, lay side by side in death. I know more about their marriage than I do about some of my own family members' marriages. There is a reason for this. This is so unusual in Scripture that it seems God is literally screaming out to us to pay attention to this. There are, of course, a multitude of theological constructs we can deduce when reading these passages and seeking God's insight. Do not think for a moment that I am suggesting the only reason these events are laid bare in the Bible is so we can see how a marriage works. There is way more complexity to it than that. I am proposing that *part* of the reason God has chosen to include so much detail about the marriage of Isaac and Rebekah is so that we can catch just a glimpse of what being married is all about. He is showing His design for that institution and how sin can seriously damage that design. He is also showing that, while sin can damage the design, it does not have to destroy it. Once I began working on the details of the Marriage Pyramid and including it in my marriage retreats, I also became keenly aware of how each level of the Pyramid was represented in the marriage of Isaac and Rebekah. Arguably the greatest love story in the Bible was rife with a combination of conflict and joy so that this amazing couple drifted up and down the scale. And that's the whole idea. We all want to be at the top, experiencing oneness and enjoying the results. But we will not stay there. We will do things on accident. We will do things on purpose. We will vacillate up and down the Pyramid. That's the whole idea of how I developed it in the first place. Again, this is not a *plan* to do so that we will stay at the top. It's a way to visualize something that we all experience but very few of us know how to process.

It is a way to evaluate where we are in our marriage relationship as God has designed it to be. It is a way to observe and evaluate what things in our marriage might be keeping us at that level at that time. What parasites are draining the life from this sacred institution? And when we have that information, it is then a very short jump to what we could do together, through God's power, to remove the barriers keeping us from an optimal marriage. Keeping us from the marriage God has designed. And keeping us from experiencing what oneness really is in light of Who God is and what He wants for us. I hope you have found this part helpful. I really do. It is the crux of the reason I wrote all of this in the first place. I hope the Pyramid makes a bit of sense in light of what I am trying to say. We've spent quite a while talking about this, and it is my sincerest prayer that it will nestle in your brain and your heart as you, hopefully, use this to get just a glimpse of a picture of what the optimal marriage looks like from God's perspective. We have finished with the Pyramid, but I want to finish the book with one more chapter that I hope will help just accentuate what we've already learned. If you've stuck with me so far, maybe you'll stick around just a bit longer.

Chapter Six
ODDS AND ENDS

I realize the name of the book is *The Marriage Pyramid*, and I know I finished up the last of the Pyramid in the last chapter, but I really did want to talk about a few more important ideas quickly (very quickly) before we part ways. I love marriage. I am passionate about marriage. While many of my comrades would often complain about the amount of marital counseling they had to do as part of their job, I never did. Not because I did not grow weary of the same issues being raised in the same arguments while ending up the same way, because I did grow weary of that at times. I say this with no joy or hint of pride at all, but I got to the point where I could generally tell whether a couple was going to make it within the first 15 minutes of the conversation. I would hear words or see faces or read attitudes so quickly (because I had seen them more often) that it did not take much for me to see whether a couple was doomed or if there was hope. And by doomed I do not necessarily mean that the couple would end up in divorce court, though that was the usual outcome. But even if they decided to stay together, I could see that it would never be a true, loving marriage where both felt safe, both wanted to grow together, and both experienced oneness. They would simply be two people living in the same house and tolerating whatever they chose to tolerate in the name of "staying together." Not that there's anything wrong with simply trying to stay together. In fact, it is an admirable trait in the culture we now inhabit. Marriage has become disposable, just like everything else. We have lost a sense of the sacred attached to this remarkable institution. It is that admiration for the sacrosanct nature of marriage as designed by God that kept me excited about helping couples for all of these years.

In a way, the idea of marriage is more important than the two adherents that make up the marriage. Make any sense? That's the way I felt then. That's the way I feel now. Marriage is such a precious commodity that I cannot help but to get excited helping people see what it can *really* be like. What God *really* intended it to be. And how the secular world has *really* hosed it up. I stated earlier that leading marriage retreats was one of the most rewarding things I did. That's where the idea of the Marriage Pyramid was born, and I got to see God work in the lives of many, many couples. But, again, it might surprise you to know that the Pyramid was only one segment of the retreats I led. It was the one most well-received, and it was the last module prior to finishing up on the second day. I am, of course, no longer in the Navy, but I am still leading marriage retreats. Right now, I am the President of a virtual discipleship ministry called Growth Project. The name implies the mission. We engage in a number of projects designed to fulfill the biblical mandate prescribed in Matthew 28 to "make disciples of all nations." You will get a better glimpse of how we do that in the last chapter. But the marriage retreats play a large role in that mission. And while we do go into some depth regarding the Pyramid, we also delve into other vitally important elements related to a healthy marriage. I mentioned earlier that I call that section "Relationship Killers." I do so because that is exactly what they are, if left unchecked.

So I did not want to leave you without at least an introduction to what these relationship killers are. If you want more detail about how they work to undermine and destroy relationships, I recommend having us come out to provide you one of our marriage retreats/seminars. For our purposes in this book, a brief introduction to these destructive practices will have to suffice.

Therefore, before we part company, let me share with you some of the most destructive relationship killers.

Unrealistic expectations. I covered this a bit earlier in the book, but I wanted to bring it up again. Why? It is a very simple answer. In my experience, with all of the crises I have heard of and witnessed, unrealistic expectations have been at the top of the list for the reasons most marriages end or end up in real trouble. Not only are unrealistic expectations a key to every single relationship you will ever have with any person or entity, they are one of *the* most important components to an optimal marriage. Simply put, I cannot expect my spouse to be more than they are capable of being. Notice, I didn't say what they *can* be. That's a totally different issue. I am a better person because my wife has encouraged me and strengthened me to be more than I ever thought possible. She shows me that I *can* be the things I am capable of being but that I doubt I can be. She compliments, encourages, challenges, and urges me on to reach my potential. That's what a spouse should do. But she knows my limitations. She knows the difference between what I can do and what I can't do. And she does not expect me to *do* the things I can't *do*. She doesn't expect me to *be* the things I cannot *be*.

I have had people sit across from me and tell me with near pride that their spouse is "my everything." I want to scream out, "NO!" Your spouse cannot be your everything because your spouse is flawed. Just like you are flawed. Look at it this way. If I expect my wife to respond to me the way I think she should, in the time period I think she should, every time I think she should, I have placed her on a pedestal. It is important to note this, however — this is not a pedestal that she requested to placed on nor is it a pedestal she would ask to remain on. I placed her on there. I didn't ask. She didn't volunteer. So let me ask you a question. My wife, being human, is going to fall from that pedestal, isn't she? Yes.

Just as I would fall from a similar perch. She will not always respond to me perfectly because she is imperfect. But I have placed her atop a perfect pedestal. So she will fall. When she falls, am I going to be mad at me for putting her up there in the first place? Or am I going to be mad at her for falling from a pedestal she didn't seek and didn't want to be on in the first place? Of course, nine times out of ten, I am going to get angry at her. I will get angry at her for falling from a place she should not have been and that I am to blame for putting her on in the first place.

What are we getting at here? Your spouse will let you down. That is realistic. Your spouse will do things that will make you angry. That is realistic. Your spouse will do things wrong. That is realistic. Your spouse will be grumpy, irrational, dismissive, and argumentative. That is realistic. Your spouse will sometimes infuriate you. That is realistic. Please don't misunderstand — this is not necessarily bad news. It actually can be very good news. Because we are all like that. There have been so many times that I have counseled couples on the brink of divorce because one or both of the spouses had unrealistic expectations of each other. It happens over and over and over again. And this is one we do not talk about enough because we are so busy focusing on the symptoms instead of the cause. I remember talking to one spouse who was frustrated with her husband to the point of divorce. But try as I might, I could not figure out how they had gotten to that point. She then uttered the magic words about her marriage: "It's not what I expected." Once I heard what she expected, I made it clear that the potential husband she just described did not nor would he ever exist because that person does not exist. We have to understand this about our spouse.

They are human. And humans do stupid, selfish things sometimes because we are wracked with sin in our life. Look, there are some universally accepted things we can realistically expect from all spouses. We can expect our spouse to not physically abuse us. We can expect our spouse not to commit adultery. We can expect our spouse not to be addicted to drugs and alcohol. We can expect our spouse not to emotionally abuse us. After that, it becomes a bit muddier. Because we are all different, with all differing strengths and weaknesses, we cannot expect our spouse to be what they are not *capable* of being. None of us are capable of being the perfect spouse. None of us are capable of doing only the things our spouse wants all the time. None of us can be responsible for making our spouse happy. Because we cannot be responsible for *anyone's* happiness. We can contribute to it, or we can detract from it, but we cannot be responsible for it. My wife is not designed to find true joy in me. Because I cannot fulfill that mandate. You are not designed to find true joy in your spouse because your spouse is not designed to fulfill that mandate. I cannot complete my wife because we are designed so that only One can really and truly complete us, and that is God.

I plead with you — give your spouse a break. I'm not talking about ignoring prolonged and continued bad behavior with little to no impetus to correct them. I'm talking about understanding that God's perfect design for marriage was immutably tainted by sin so that we will never completely experience what marriage was originally intended to be. But we can still have an optimal marriage. We can still have the experience of what it means to be one with one another because of the grace that God bestows on us without measure. Realize that your spouse is just a frail, tainted person trying to love you and that you are just as frail and tainted. When we start expecting of our spouses only what they are capable of giving us, then we will take a tool out of the Enemy's hands that he uses to bludgeon marriages into submission. Your spouse has issues. You have issues. That perfect family down the street or that you see plastered across Facebook has issues. How do I know this?

Because "the heart is deceitful above all things, and desperately wicked; Who can know it?" (Jeremiah 17:9 NKJV). You married someone with a wicked heart. Your spouse married someone with a wicked heart. Now do you see why only God can grant the power to become one in marriage? Only He and His forgiveness of sin allows us to even have a shot at this miraculous institution. But we have to always remember to keep our expectations about our spouse realistic. This is incredibly important in order to keep that relationship killer away from your marriage.

Catastrophic statements/anger/arguing. People are going to argue. It seems that has become a spectator sport in our culture today. I get it. I really do. But we would at least try our best to protect our marriage relationship from arguing if we had a proper understanding of the essence of an argument. The best way to begin is by asking a very simple question. If you get this wrong, then you miss why arguments are so devastating to a marriage. Here is the question: what is the goal of an argument? Think about it carefully before you answer and really think about it. What is the goal of an argument? The answer: to win. If you had any other answer than this one, then you are in grave danger of underestimating the role that arguing plays in a marriage. Remember, we just finished talking about unrealistic expectations, and this is a good case in point. It is completely unrealistic to think that you and your spouse will not argue. You will most certainly argue. However, you must never get comfortable with the idea of arguing or assume that arguments are anything other than one person trying to defeat the other. The goal of an argument is to win the argument. And if one person has to win, the other person has to lose. And if there is one constant in human nature (especially in America), we hate to lose. I used to ask this question in the retreats every time we got to the section on relationship killers. It never failed that one of the most common answers I got to that very important question was, "The goal of an argument is to work things out." Really? Is that what happens in an argument? We argue with our spouse to work things out? Now, to be sure, many times things do get worked out. But they get worked out in the *aftermath* of an argument, once things have settled down a bit. However, once things are settled down, the conversation can then no longer rightfully be called an argument. Go ahead. Argue. You're going to anyway. But always remember what the goal is in that scenario. You are pitted against your spouse, and you are both trying to win. Just understand that, and let it be a pathway to fixing disagreements.

Notice, disagreements are not the same as arguments. Disagreements can, of course (but don't *have* to), lead to arguments. In and of themselves, however, they are not the same constructs. After knowing each other for more than 46 years and having been married for nearly 30 years, there are still a number of things with which my bride and I disagree. In fact, I would lay very good odds that we will never completely agree on these (relatively speaking) fairly small things. Early in our marriage, it was not uncommon for these disagreements to devolve into regular arguments. Do you want to know why? Because we really believed that being married meant that we would always see things the same way. That, my friend, is a textbook case of an unrealistic expectation. We thought the definition of harmony in the household was the reality that we would see eye to eye on basically everything. This, of course, led to significant discourse and arguing. However, the goal of the arguing was to convince the other person they were wrong. The goal was to emerge victorious. The goal was not to agree to disagree or to acknowledge that people (even married people) can feel pretty different about a lot of things, and that's ok. Now, some 30 years later, we still do not agree on these things. But we also don't try to win an argument about them at the expense of the other person. So argue if you want, but always know what the actual goal is and use it to move onto a real way to come to a realistic conclusion to these issues.

One of the main reasons why arguing is detrimental to a marriage relationship is because arguing includes anger. And anger is a relationship killer. I'm not talking about getting a little ticked off at some sort of annoying behavior. I'm talking about real anger. The reason people do not respect the power anger has in a marriage is because they do not know the physiology behind anger. I have to admit, this information was given to me by a doctor friend who made this subject sort of a hobby. He explained it like this. When we get really angry, the body begins to react to that anger. Almost immediately, adrenaline is released into the body, and the body begins to react as if there is a threat nearby. When this threat response is triggered, the body does what it does naturally. It prepares itself to engage the so-called fight or flight response. When a significant threat causes this to happen, there are physiological effects on the body that are very palpable and very germane to this subject. Once the fight or flight response is triggered, the body begins to automatically move blood to the major muscle groups, specifically the arms, legs, and chest. This gets us ready to fight if it is in our best interest to do so or flee if it's in our best interest to do so.

Now, the body has no idea what the threat is. It is only doing what comes natural. In other words, the body doesn't know if it's doing all of this because we are angry with our spouse or if it is because a bear is chasing us through the woods. Its only job is to prepare us by moving blood to the major muscle groups we just mentioned. Here is the interesting part. The body has a finite amount of blood in it at any given time. In fact, the human body has about one and a half gallons of blood in it. Remember, the body during this process moves more blood to the necessary muscles. But since there is a static amount of blood, and it doesn't create more, it borrows blood from other parts of the body. You have one guess as to what part of the body the necessary blood is borrowed from first. Right: the brain. Therefore, think about this. At the time that you are the angriest at your spouse, you are thinking the least. The angrier you are, the less your brain is working. Even the justice system recognizes this reality. Premeditated, first-degree murder is charged more severely and penalized more aggressively than killings done "in the heat of passion." This is done because the justice system realizes that people will do things in the heat of passion that they might not have normally done. That's why we say and do the most horrendous things to our spouse when we're angry and then genuinely feel sorrow for those things after the fact. But by then, the damage is done. And the things have been said and done, never to be forgotten. Forgiven? Maybe. But never forgotten. Anger is a key component to arguing, and that's why it has to be understood as a relationship killer. That's why it must be avoided as much as is feasible.

One of the ways to do that? Stop making catastrophic statements to your spouse. We will not beat this probably-wounded horse any more than necessary, since we did talk about this earlier. But it bears repeating. Catastrophic statements are statements made by a spouse that unfairly characterizes the other spouse and is patently untrue at its core. It's not always the case, but the vast majority of catastrophic statements begin with the words "you always" and/or "you never." It does not matter what sentence comes after one of those two preambles — it is guaranteed to be a lie. No one always does something. No one never does something else. If you say to your spouse, "you always complain," that is a lie. If you say to your spouse, "you never help around the house," that is a lie. You may *feel* that way at the time, as your anger and frustration grows, but we've talked about feelings. They are not an arbiter for the veracity of a truth claim. Your frustration may, in fact, be justified. However, your engaging in a lie to make your point is not. It will not get you anywhere but into a deeper argument with even more anger involved. When you use those phrases, you are lying about your spouse, and people do *not* like being lied about by anyone, much less their spouse. That then becomes a safety issue within the Pyramid (as does anger, by the way) and will keep you from experiencing the oneness God has for your marriage. We are all guilty of this. We all have done it. We've gotten too comfortable doing it. And we've got to stop. It will generate anger and arguing and guarantee that you are actually *inviting* these relationship killers into your marriage. The Adversary already wants these things to be present in your relationship. Don't help him by welcoming them in yourself.

Forgiveness. Lastly, we will end here, where I end all of my retreats. I want this to be the last thing a married couple hears before they leave the sanctity of the retreat environment and head back into the "real" world. Every single couple who has come to me for premarital counseling gets the same advice: "If you're not willing to forgive your spouse, don't get married." This is not hyperbole, and it is not stated for shock value. It is simply the truth. Because every single spouse on the planet is going to do something wrong, every single spouse is going to need forgiveness. Every single spouse is going to have to ask for forgiveness. Every single spouse is going to have to ask to be forgiven. We are all in this together. Forgiveness is as necessary to a marriage as breathing is to a body. It removes bad air from a relationship by infusing it with new, good, refreshing air. We are all going to do things wrong. Sometimes on accident. Sometimes on purpose. But we will do something to hurt our spouse in some way, shape, or form. That is a realistic expectation. And that's the bad news. The good news is that it doesn't have to stay hurt. Just as our fractured relationship with God is healed via forgiveness, so can our relationship with our spouse. It may not be easy. In fact, it probably won't be, depending on the issue. But it is good. It is healing. And it is freeing in a way most people cannot imagine.

That doesn't mean that there aren't some misunderstandings about the nature of forgiveness. While we don't have the time to go into detail (come to the retreat!) about this vital component of marriage, we can quickly look at a few misconceptions. For one, forgiveness is not forgetting. Forgetting is dementia. If you have an expectation that forgiveness means both the forgiver and the forgivee will somehow experience forgetting that the offense ever took place, that is an unrealistic expectation. I can remember hurtful things my wife said to me more than 30 years ago. She remembers hurtful things I said to her more than 30 years ago. But remembering those things does *not* mean that we have not forgiven each other. Painful things are painful for a reason. And they leave an indelible mark. So it is only natural and realistic to expect that they will cross our mind from time to time. Also, the more hurtful the offense, the more that memory will linger and the more we may still mourn it. Even after forgiveness is extended. Which leads to another misconception.

Forgiveness does not mean letting the offender off the hook or not ever talking about the event again. Once more, the more hurtful the offense, the truer this becomes. A breach of trust like adultery is going to have a longer shelf life than yelling at your spouse for leaving no gas in the car. They both need to be dealt with. They both need forgiveness. They both will linger. But one will linger far longer and have more ramifications than the other. What often happens is that the more devastating the event, the more the offended needs to work through it, even after offering forgiveness. This can be confusing for the offender. Using the adultery example again, the offended spouse may offer forgiveness but still need to bring it up from time to time as they continue to mourn the event. The offender has to see that this is not a sign of lack of forgiveness but that the offense was so grievous that it will take a while to work through, even in the aftermath of forgiveness. However, if you've forgiven your spouse and you bring that event up when you find yourself in a one-down position where you need to be forgiven, that's an entirely different story. That will always be seen as your claim of forgiveness being a lie. However, just because you need to talk about and get through an event that was very painful doesn't mean you haven't forgiven someone.

Forgiveness is also *not* a feeling. It is a decision. It is a decision that you will no longer hold that offense to that person's account. They do not "owe" you, and they will not have to "pay" for what they have done. I have lost track of the number of people I have counseled over the years who have come to me doubting their forgiveness. It's interesting what people will ask you when you're in the role of a counselor. I have actually had folks ask *me* if *they've* forgiven someone. Interesting, isn't it? But I understand the question. The question is based, in large part, on the person linking actual forgiveness with the feelings they assume should be a part of forgiveness. Once again (it's amazing how often this comes up), how we feel about our decision and effort to forgive someone is not the litmus test on whether we have actually forgiven that person. This is closely linked with the misconception we just discussed. People will doubt they have forgiven because they still feel pain over the event. They doubt they have forgiven because they still feel sad or bad about the person who harmed them. They doubt they have forgiven because the event is as fresh in their mind as if it happened yesterday. However, that is a false dichotomy they have constructed in their minds. Forgiving and remembering are not mutually exclusive. Many times (I would say most times), we are not going to feel "good" about the event we have forgiven. It just simply doesn't work that way. That's why forgiveness is a conscious decision to no longer hold that event against that particular person, regardless of how much that offense may have hurt us. Simply put, feelings don't count for much when it comes to forgiveness. Decide to forgive, and you are on your way to doing so.

Lastly, and quickly, there are a couple of other things that must be mentioned when trying to understand this construct. People may decide to forgive and elect not to continue on with the relationship with their spouse. It is sad when that happens, but it does happen. If a person is in an abusive relationship with a spouse and wants to forgive said spouse, by all means do so. But that doesn't mean that you should stay in that abusive relationship. Remember, forgiveness does not mean that you are absolving the offender from their personal responsibility for their offense. There is a price to pay for sin. And though, if you are a Believer, God will not hold you eternally responsible for sin, He does allow temporal consequences for our actions. If a spouse is an abuser, you may elect to forgive the abuser. But it would be the height of foolishness to stay with the abuser. If your spouse is a serial philanderer, you may elect to forgive the philanderer. But it would be the height of foolishness to stay with the philanderer. This, of course, hinges on whether there is genuine repentance of these actions and whether you believe, as best you can, that this behavior will not happen again. Forgiveness does not mean that you have to keep the offender in your life in any way, shape, or form. Nor should you, if they do not seek the forgiveness or acknowledge their offense. So forgiveness is not inextricably linked to staying in the relationship.

Also (and this is important to remember), forgiveness is more for the one forgiving than it is for the one receiving the forgiveness. I mentioned in the above paragraph the idea that there could be people who have harmed you in your life and who refuse to acknowledge that harm or ask for forgiveness. That is not a lynchpin for forgiveness. Many times, people in our lives have been harmed by people who could care less whether we forgive them or not, simply because they do not believe themselves to be responsible for the pain. Or worse, they could not care that they cause us pain. In those circumstances, forgiveness is difficult for some and downright impossible for others. That's why Scripture tells us to forgive as Christ forgave us (Ephesians 4:32). One of the most interesting aspects of that idea is that Jesus forgave us when He considered us His enemies (Romans 5:10). His forgiveness was not dependent on an acknowledgement that we were His enemies. For us, forgiving the "unforgivable" is way more beneficial to us than it is to them. Withholding forgiveness takes effort. It takes energy. It takes anger. And it takes hatred. All of that takes a toll on us. What toll does it take on the person we are refusing to forgive? None. They don't care in the first place. And if they do start out caring, after a very short amount of time of being reminded that they are not going to be forgiven, they quickly begin to not care. So the pain that you may have thought you were inflicting on them by withholding forgiveness vanishes in the air of ambivalence. The only thing that remains is the pain you are inflicting on yourself by withholding forgiveness. Therefore, if you want to view forgiveness as a selfish thing so that you care more about how it frees you than it does them, I'm all for that. I am a pragmatist, if nothing else.

The important takeaway here is that forgiveness is absolutely essential to the marriage relationship and that misunderstanding it opens a pathway to these relationship killers. That's the whole reason for this chapter in the first place. If you're reading this and wishing I would have gone into more detail regarding these relationship killers, I suggest two things. First, this is a book primarily about the Marriage Pyramid, and I didn't want to dilute that message with other important (but slightly off topic) constructs. Second, come to the marriage retreat! These retreats are a vital part of the ministry I have engaged in, both while in the Navy and now afterwards. There are so many details that have been left out of this entire paradigm because I have chosen to focus on just one part of the retreat, the Pyramid. I cannot tell you how much I learn about what it means to be married in the eyes of the Designer of marriage every time I lead one of these retreats. I feel both more inadequate and more encouraged each and every single time. I know I will fall short as a husband. But I also know that, in Him, I can be the husband He has called me to be. If I'm lucky, maybe I'll get real good at this marriage thing in another 20 years or so.

So that's it. We have reached the end of our journey. I really want this to have been a worthwhile journey. But I hope and pray (actually, pray more than hope) that it is just the beginning of the journey God has for you and your spouse. That is true whether you've been married 5 years or 55 years. God created marriage. He wants you to **love** in the way that He loves. He wants you to be **safe** with your spouse in every way imaginable. He wants you to grow in Him so that you can and will **grow** with each other. He wants you to experience **oneness** that can only be found in Him and can only be shared with one person on the planet — your spouse. Here's wishing you the very best marriage you can possibly have. The marriage God intended for you to have. How cool is that?

Chapter Seven
GROWTH PROJECT

Here at Growth Project, the entire focus of all that we do is to make disciples. Throughout Christendom, churches and para-church organizations have done a relatively good job of leading people to Christ. We have done a less good job of making disciples. There are pockets of success out there, but the reality is that, theologically-speaking, the vast majority of Believers in this country today are a mile wide and an inch deep. They do not know what they believe or why it's true. This has contributed, to a large extent, to the reason that so many younger Believers now hold cultural and social views that mirror the secular world and directly contradict Biblical truth.

All of this, despite the rapid rise of megachurches. According to Christianity Today, "There are as many megachurches today in the greater Nashville area as there were in the entire country in 1960." Yet, despite the plethora of megachurches who baptize regularly and add congregants by the hundreds (or even thousands) nationwide, church attendance has been in decline for decades. People seem to be entering the front door of the church through (hopefully) effective evangelism and then leaving through the church's back door due to a lack of growth. We here at Growth Project, through our lack of action, have been, in one way or another, a part of that problem. We now want to be part of the solution.

That is why everything we will do here at Growth Project is poured through the filter of discipleship. How do we know Him better, and how is what we are doing helping us reach that goal? Those are the questions we have to answer before we make any decision and initiate any program. Simply put: we are here to know Him and to make Him known by rooting all that we do in His Word. Here, we are steadfastly committed to growing disciples by rooting them in God's Word. Everything that we do here at Growth Project is designed with two simple foundational elements: to know Him and to make Him known. These are the filters through which we pour every idea and decision. We always ask the question: "How does this help me know Him better?" As a result of that question, we have developed four areas of concentration that we strongly feel will obey the mandate given to us by Christ: to make disciples.

EDUCATING PEOPLE (Ro. 12:2)

The first area of concentration is: Educating People. This will entail more formal educational processes to impart the theological and intellectual knowledge necessary to know Him better. Usually these types of opportunities are available only to those who are attending seminary. Our goal is to develop a "lay" seminary that people can access from their homes, if they so choose. We will include such endeavors as: classes on subjects like systematic theology, apologetics and worldview, and hermeneutics. We are also working on an introductory theology companion reader designed to go along with a book of the Bible. The key phrase here is: formal training available to all Believers.

ENHANCING LIVES (Hosea 4:6)

Our second area of concentration is: Enhancing Lives. This will be the practical application of the truths discovered through formal study. The idea here is to present material that will help the average Believer see and live out the truths of God's Word to enhance their walk with the Lord so that we can be the disciples He wants us to be. We have many of these strategies in place right now. The Bible Support Group and the accompanying Growth Project Radio sessions we do weekly are already up and running. We also produce "5 Minutes of Truth," a group of short podcasts, devotional in nature, that provide God's truth in bite-sized morsels. Other endeavors include our regular Marriage Seminars and other enhancing opportunities.

EQUIPPING OTHERS (Acts 18:26)

We do not want to be the only folks doing this, because we can't be. This area will focus on us being available to help other organizations design and implement their own Growth Project via training, consulting, and leadership development. Our vision is to see other churches and/or para-church organizations developing their own Growth Project organizations to facilitate discipleship in their own communities. We want to multiply what we are doing to benefit all Believers. Therefore, we have developed a systematic and teachable way to train organizations to implement the strategies we formulated but in ways unique to their own theological and organizational cultures. Our most popular training endeavor is the Discipleship Development Program designed to teach churches and para-church organizations to to develop virtual discipleship strategies.

ENGAGING THE ARTS (Eph. 2:10)

We have our friends over at **renewthearts.org** for this one. Throughout history, the arts have been used to communicate God's truth, His grace, and His love for us. We endeavor to keep that tradition alive. This area will focus on allowing artists to use their medium, in whatever way God calls them to, in order to further the Gospel. This will take the forms of short films, fiction, essays, and poetry. These will be produced in-house, as well as from submitted works from outside sources. We also plan to partner with like-minded ministries and organizations in order to provide a platform for artists, who are also Believers, to communicate God's truth via a medium that speaks to millions of people.

If you are interested in engaging with us to provide activities that reinforce any of these core competencies in your own church or para-church organization, please reach out to us. We are available to provide marriage retreats, leadership training, virtual discipleship training modules, and a variety of other discipleship-based endeavors. Please feel free to reach out to us for more information. We have a variety of resources and services we can offer to help you and your organization make and grow disciples. We offer training and leadership programs along with marriage retreats/conferences including many of the constructs in this book.

Our website is at www.growthproject.org. Let us know how we can serve alongside you.

BIO

Dr. Danny Purvis is a veteran of the United States Navy where he spent 20 years as a Chaplain. He has counseled hundreds of married couples under the most challenging circumstances. Dr. Purvis has also led dozens of marriage retreats as the director of the Navy's marriage retreat program. The Marriage Pyramid was born and nurtured during the two decades he spent helping marriages be the best they could possibly be. He has been married to his bride, Kimberly, for nearly 30 years and together they have raised four children. They currently reside in Central Florida.

www.ingramcontent.com/pod-product-compliance
Lightning Source LLC
LaVergne TN
LVHW052025080426
835513LV00018B/2159